ROBERT A. M. STERN

ROBERT A. M. STERN

Buildings and Projects
1999–2003

Edited by Peter Morris Dixon

THE MONACELLI PRESS

First published in the United States of America
in 2003 by
The Monacelli Press, Inc.
902 Broadway, New York, New York 10010.

Library of Congress Cataloging-in-Publication
Data
Stern, Robert A. M.
Robert A. M. Stern : buildings and projects,
1999/2003.
p.   cm.
Includes bibliographical references.
ISBN 1-58093-121-9 (hardcover)—
ISBN 1-58093-122-7 (pbk.)
1. Stern, Robert A. M. 2. Robert A. M. Stern
Architects. 3. Architecture—United States—
20th century. I. Title.
NA737.S64A4   2003
720'.92—dc22   2003017186

Front cover: Gap Inc. Offices at Two Folsom
Street, San Francisco, California. Sculpture:
Charlie Brown by Richard Serra. Photograph:
Peter Aaron/Esto.

Back cover: Smith Campus Center, Pomona
College, Claremont, California. Photograph:
Peter Aaron/Esto.

Printed and bound in Italy

Designed by Abigail Sturges

Contents

Introduction

Robert A. M. Stern

Architecture is the art of the possible and the contingent. It is an enabling art, an art of affirmation and reaffirmation. Every circumstance of daily life—a sunlit corner in a courtyard, a glimpse of nature in a dense urban setting—has within it a magic capable of transforming mere building into place-making, of helping lift lives to higher levels of awareness while dignifying the daily routine. Our job—the job of all architects—is to bring forth this magic from the mundane, to create settings for ordinary events and for those moments of ritual, reflection, and revelation that are essential to lives well lived.

These are difficult but interesting times for the profession, as the age-old authority of built form is challenged by the immense imagistic power of electronic media, which some architects find so compelling that they are prepared to overthrow architecture as we know it. But despite the razzle-dazzle of electronics and projective imagery, I remain convinced that built architecture—that is, permanent, not virtual, architecture—remains of paramount importance. It must be valued for what it is, has been, and will always be: an enduring public record of who we are, who we were, and who we hope to become. Though new times need new solutions, architecture has the obligation to see beyond the moment as it remains true to its own nature and purpose. The great challenge to the architect is not just to have an idea, a vision, but to develop that vision into something tangible, useful, of enduring value.

Architecture is perhaps the last stronghold for humanism, the last discipline dedicated to the celebration of the intellectual and cultural traits that permit men and women to coexist, to communicate, to share. A building only truly succeeds as a work of architecture when it is adopted by a wide range of people and becomes a part of a common experience, when it connects with culture as a whole. It will be too bad if we too easily succumb to the siren song of electronics only to realize that we have traded a physical architecture of solid and void for an illusionistic world of smoke, mirrors, mist, and fog.

Our firm welcomes new ideas, and we cherish ideas from the past. We welcome debate, even disagreement; we think and reflect; yet we remain dedicated to our primary purpose: to build. We believe that everything is possible, but that not everything is right. While we enjoy the ebbs and flows of fashion, we are committed to the fertile common ground that nourishes and refreshes a lifetime of work in architecture. There are many ways of making architecture, and there will be many more—the human capacity for imagination and invention is limitless—but at the core certain standards must define quality. It is necessary to take risks to thrive as an architect—but not at the expense of basic core values. To ignore the basics is not to make art out of the act of building but to condemn architecture to infantilism.

Architecture is construction, context, and so much more: a culture, a commitment, a lifelong path to the discovery of the new and to the rediscovery of the forgotten. This monograph of the recent work of our firm documents five years of the efforts of a collaborative venture that has lasted more than thirty. While I am proud to be the leader of this effort, it is not by any means mine alone: it is a partnership of talents dedicated to ideals.

Architecture is not some trivial pursuit. It is a vital natural force, an important human activity, a constellation of possibilities; it is the best way humankind has yet devised to shape the world.

Buildings and Projects
1999–2003

Residence

Chestnut Hill, Massachusetts
1986–1991

12   At the crest of a hill at the end of a long drive that winds across a recently subdivided estate, this hipped-roof house, embraced by wings and flanking pavilions, evokes the Adamesque classicism of nearby houses including the Gore Mansion in Waltham (1806), although in many ways a more immediate source for the composition is George Howe's house, High Hollow, in the Chestnut Hill section of Philadelphia (1914).

The motor court begins an axial sequence that leads past the principal stair hall and dining room to the groin-vaulted living room, which commands a view across a long sloping meadow. Daylight descending from a rooftop monitor marks the cross axis, where one of a pair of stairs leads down to a grass terrace that widens as it passes a gazebo and approaches the rolling lawn. The wings contain more informal living spaces as well as a gentle ramp that leads past the field house, then turns and continues to the game room and swimming pool below.

1. *Garden facade*
   from southwest
2. *Entrance facade*
   from north

   Overleaf
3. *Garden facade*
   from west

1, 2

4. Monitor and
   entrance hall
5. Entrance hall
   looking to stair

4

6. Second-floor plan
7. First-floor plan
8. Ground-floor plan
9. Living room looking to
   entrance hall

18

6

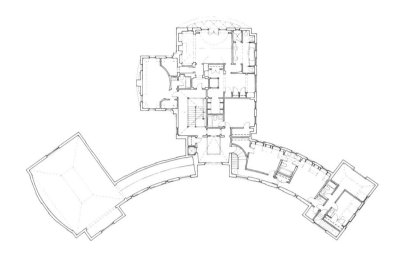

7

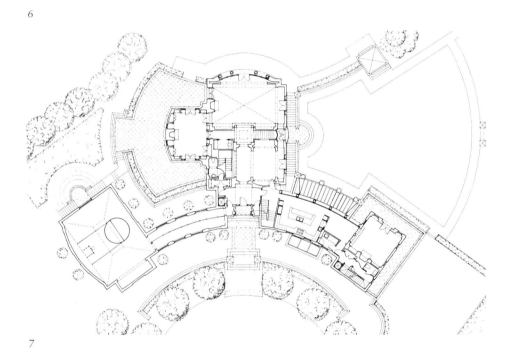

0   10   20   40 ft

8

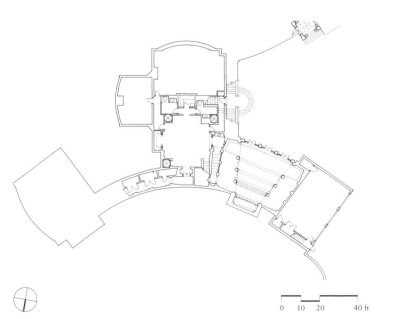

10

11, 12

14, 15

Gap Inc. Offices at Two Folsom Street

San Francisco, California
1992–2001

1. Ground-floor
   plan
2. Site plan
3. Location plan
4. Embarcadero
   entrance from
   northeast

26 Occupying a prominent site of nearly two acres facing San Francisco Bay, this building aims at once to be part of its neighborhood of warehouses and industrial buildings and to provide an icon on the city's skyline. To this end, we coupled a cubical background mass, recalling the adjacent Hills Bros. warehouse, with a slender foreground tower that takes its cue from the nearby Ferry Terminal Building at the foot of Market Street. Tawny French limestone, matching precast concrete, and red brick cloak the pared-down facades, which are punctuated by the simple structural frames of the entrance porticos and of the boldly scaled tower.

Inside, a seven-story atrium capped with a skylight of translucent laminated glass contains artist Richard Serra's sixty-foot-tall sculpture *Charlie Brown*, which was commissioned expressly for the building. Ringed by open balconies, the atrium brings natural light into the heart of the building's first six large office floors. The seventh floor—the first tower floor—houses an employee dining room and fitness center that open onto a roof garden designed in association with the Olin Partnership.

Two Folsom Street is an exemplar of environmentally sustainable design. The 540,000-square-foot building features operable windows (unusual in recent high-rise construction) as well as an underfloor air-supply system that takes advantage of the building's thermal mass to reduce peak cooling loads. Both the atrium and the ten-foot-eight-inch ceilings bring natural light deep into the building's interior.

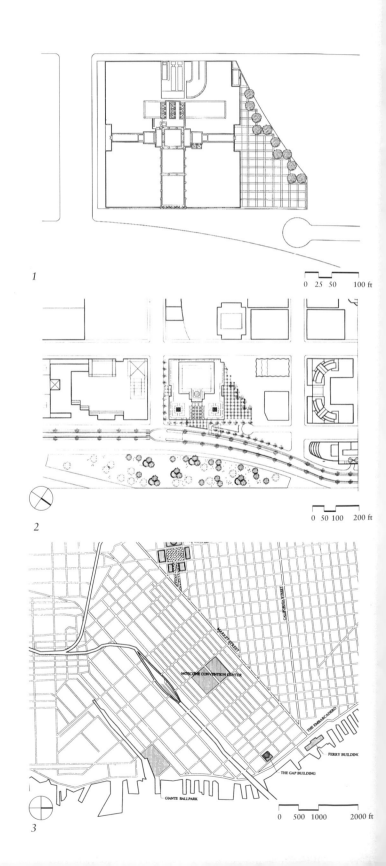

1

0 25 50   100 ft

2

0 50 100   200 ft

3

0 500 1000   2000 ft

5

6

9. *Roof garden from above*
10. *Roof garden from southeast*
11. *View from roof garden to San Francisco–Oakland Bay Bridge*

9

10

12. *Atrium skylights
with tower above*
13. *Atrium looking
east*
14. *Richard Serra's
Charlie Brown
in the atrium*

12

13

15

16

15. *Double-height gallery at Folsom Street entrance*
16. *Double-height gallery at security desk and lobby*
17. *Security desk and lobby*

17

18. Embarcadero
    entrance
19. View from
    San Francisco Bay

Overleaf
20. View from north

18

19

Residence

Kings Point, New York
1992–1997

44   Commanding a bluff overlooking Long Island Sound, this picturesque house is oriented to take advantage of dramatic views of City Island and the Manhattan skyline. Hip-roofed wings frame a gambrelled central volume and a motor court, which is anchored at the center by a porte cochere. Evoking the lighthouses of the North Shore, a two-and-a-half-story tower, complete with Fresnel lens, concludes the composition.

Behind the prominent east gable, a double-height stair hall is lighted by an oriel window. Inside the central volume on the first floor, the principal rooms, including living room, library, and dining room, are organized in an enfilade. The master suite and children's bedrooms are on the second floor. On the water side, a generous covered porch shades the house from the afternoon sun; toward the north, the porch breaks free from the main mass of the house and extends outward as a gently curving screened area with multiple exposures.

0 50 100   200 ft

2

3, 4

Previous pages
1. *Entrance (east)*
   facade

2. *Site plan*
3. *South facade*
4. *View from northwest*
5. *Porch*

6

6. *Enfilade from dining room*
7. *First-floor plan*
8. *Gallery and living room*
9. *Second-floor plan*

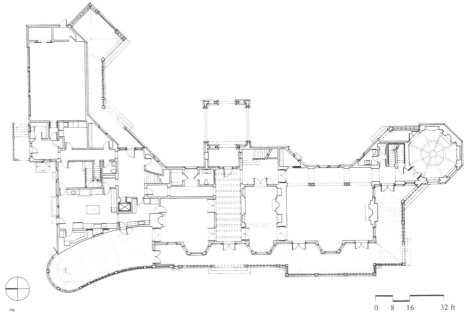

7

0 8 16   32 ft

8

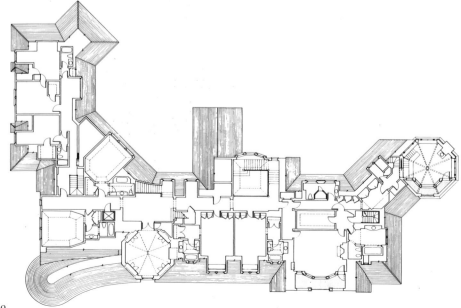

9

10

10. Entry hall
11. Lower study
12. Stair hall

11

13

14

Moore Psychology Building
Dartmouth College

Hanover, New Hampshire
1992–1999

56   Establishing the first corner in Dartmouth College's new North Campus Quadrangle, this four-story, hundred-thousand-square-foot red-brick and limestone building provides faculty offices and laboratories in separate wings linked by a core of meeting rooms, seminar and colloquium rooms, and lounges, which promote spontaneous intellectual interaction between faculty and students. Though the labs are state-of-the-art, the character of the building is not clinical but collegiate, with extensive use of oak paneling in the public rooms, and complements Dartmouth's traditional palette of red brick, Indiana limestone, and New Hampshire granite.

0   40   80   160 ft

1

3. View from south
4. Laboratory wing
   facade detail

3, 4

5

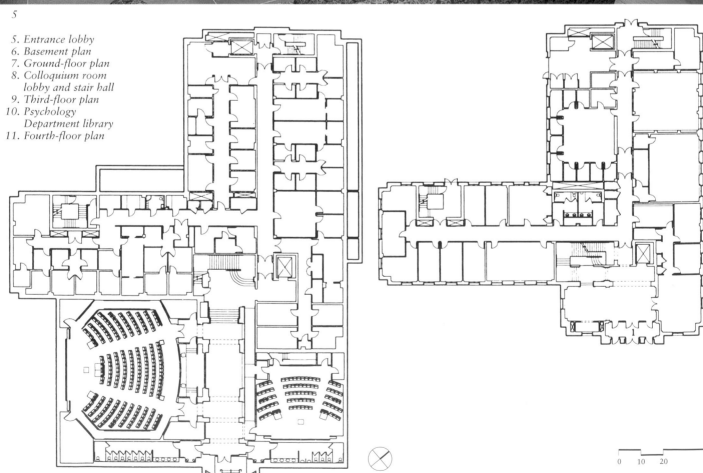

5. Entrance lobby
6. Basement plan
7. Ground-floor plan
8. Colloquium room
   lobby and stair hall
9. Third-floor plan
10. Psychology
    Department library
11. Fourth-floor plan

0 10 20   40 ft

6   7

8

10

9

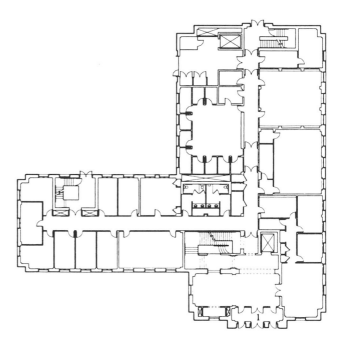

11

12

12. Filene Auditorium
13. Neurophysiology
    teaching laboratory
14. Colloquium room

    Overleaf
15. Lobby and opening
    to stair hall

13

14

16. North and east
facades from
Maynard Street
17. View from
fourth-floor
conference room

16, 17

North Campus Master Plan
Dartmouth College

Hanover, New Hampshire
Competition, 2001

1. *Existing conditions*
2. *Proposed plan*
3. *Aerial view from*
   south
4. *Dining hall from*
   south

68 Following the completion of our Moore Psychology Building (1999), Dartmouth held a design competition to plan for the long-range development of a number of linked sites north of its recently renovated and expanded Baker-Berry Library, sites currently occupied by parking lots, fraternity houses, outmoded and historic buildings, converted private residences, a historic church, and the Moore Building. In order to meet the needs for new student residences and dining halls as well as for facilities for the sciences, we proposed buildings and quadrangles that derived their stylistic vocabulary from the best of Dartmouth's existing structures.

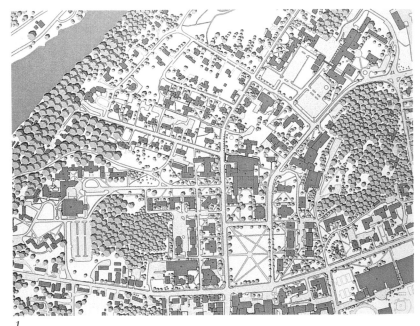

1

2

0   200   400   800 ft

3

4

Residence in
Preston Hollow

Dallas, Texas
1993–2000

1

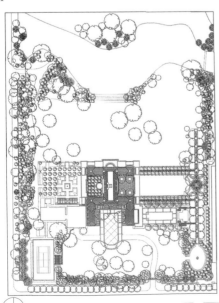

2

0 25 50   100 ft

3

4

Located in one of the older residential
neighborhoods in Dallas, this limestone-
trimmed, red-brick, slate-roofed house
is organized around exterior courtyards
that extend into the landscape. An axial
sequence leads from the square motor
court through the centrally located living
room to the lawn and creek at the south
of the site. The wings contain more
informal spaces and extensive athletic
facilities.

6. *East garden*
7. *North facade from magnolia ellipse*
8. *Lawn terrace and west facade from west allée fountain*

6

7

8

9. *Main stair*
10. *Entry hall*

9

10

11. Conservatory
12. Breakfast room
13. Dining room
   from conservatory

11, 12

14. *Living room*
15. *Second-floor plan*
16. *First-floor plan*

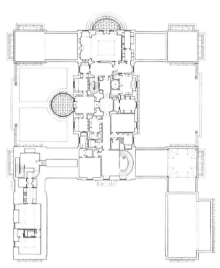

14, 15

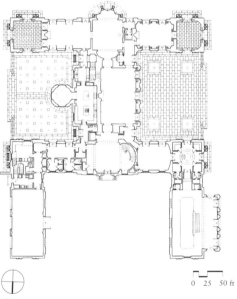

16

0   25   50 ft

17

18

20. Spa
21. Indoor pool

20

21

22. *Billiard room*
23. *West facade*
    of pool room
    from end of
    outdoor pool

22

23

Residence in Montecito

Santa Barbara, California
1993–1999

88　This geometrically disciplined villa is set at the top of a restored Italianate garden created in the 1920s. Grass parterres and a monumental allée of deodar cedars frame distant views of the Pacific Ocean. To the north, at the foot of Mount Montecito, the entry court is carved out of the hillside; a new retaining wall incorporates fountains in niches to start the sequence of water cascades that are the great glory of the restored garden.

Principal rooms are grouped around a paved courtyard with a low fountain. The more casual family rooms are clustered around a pool terrace overlooking a spectacular stone pine and the valley beyond. To the west, a screening room is set into the hill, its roof forming a grass terrace opening off the library, its single exposed facade suggesting a boathouse at the edge of an artificial pond. A guest house overlooking a tennis court makes a rustic hilltop aerie, in contrast to the formal main house.

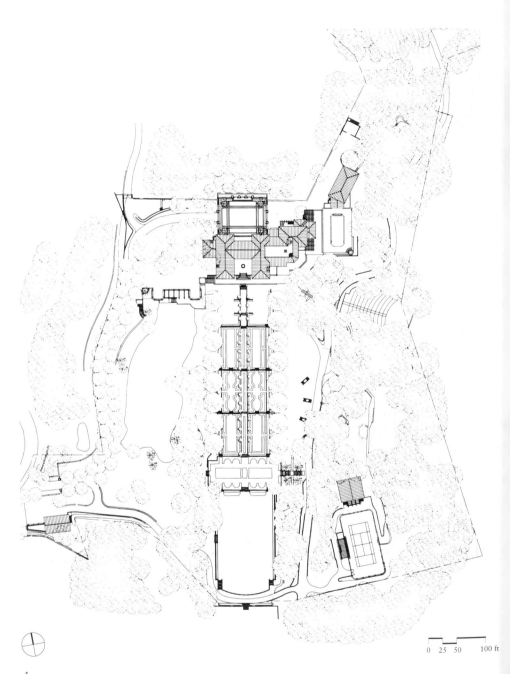

1

0　25　50　　100 ft

3

3. *North (entry) facade*
4. *Motor court from*
   entry porch

5

6

8

9

11

11. *Dining porch*
12. *Ground-floor plan*
13. *Living room looking southeast*
14. *Second-floor plan*

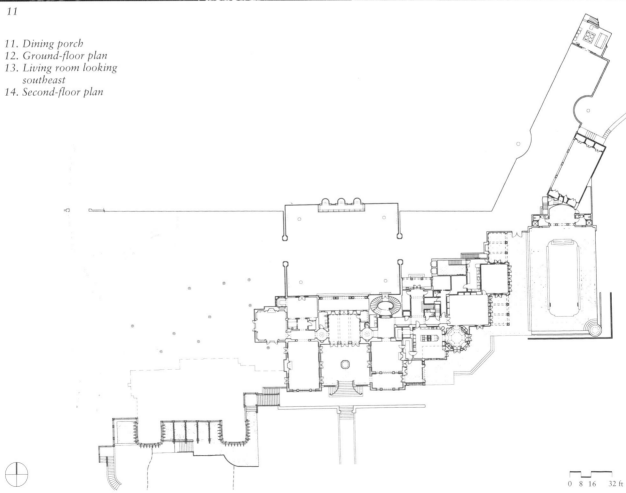

0 8 16   32 ft

13

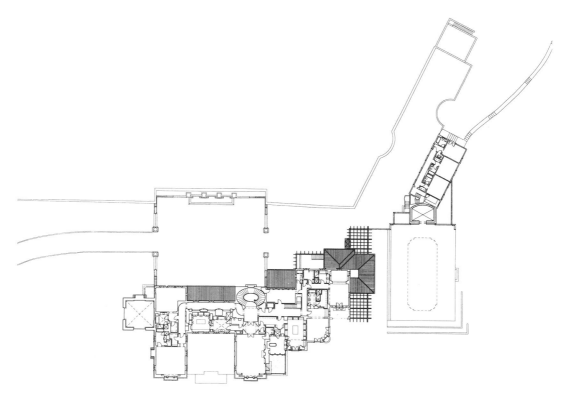

14

17

Residence at North York

Toronto, Ontario, Canada
1993–1998

106   This house occupies a small site in an established suburb. Outdoor rooms complement those within: a stone-paved motor court in the front, an enfilade of distinctly defined gardens in the back. The exterior takes its cues from some of the older houses in the surrounding neighborhood and, more significantly, from the French Norman–inspired houses of such American architects as Ernest Flagg, Robert Rodes McGoodwin, and George Howe; Howe's High Hollow inspired the pedimented central dormer high above the entrance. The steeply pitched slate roofs, rough stone walls, and discrete but interdependent pavilions and bays break down the scale of what is a deceptively large house. The complex interior spaces are organized around a double-height, handkerchief-vaulted, lantern-lighted stair hall.

1. *First-floor plan*
2. *North (entry) facade and motor court*

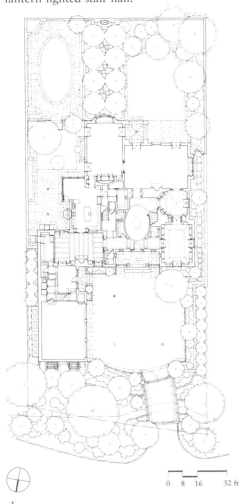

0 8 16   32 ft

1

2

3

5. *Living room
pergola and porch*
6. *Detail of south
facade*
7. *Garden allée
looking to dining
room*

5, 6

7

8. Pool court and wall
9. Garden allée and
    fountain from
    dining room
10. Pool court

8

9

10

11. *North wall of dining room from living room*
12. *Stair hall from entry*

11

Smith Campus Center
Pomona College

Claremont, California
1993–1999

1. *View from south*
2. *View from Stover Walk and Marston Quadrangle*
3. *Site plan*

118   Replacing a woefully inadequate facility constructed in 1940 and expanded in the early 1970s, the seventy-thousand-square-foot Smith Campus Center, which incorporates the 1930 Art Deco–style Edmunds Ballroom, respects Myron Hunt's 1913 plan for the Pomona campus as well as his architectural language of pavilions linked by arcades, initiated with his Little Bridges Hall, directly across Marston Quadrangle from our site. Open-air arcades reduce the amount of weather-conditioned space. The high level of detailing and materials—exposed cast-in-place board-formed reinforced-concrete walls with simple cast-stone detailing and industrial steel windows, barrel-tile roof, heavy timber pergola, deeply shaded loggias—reflects the campus's second generation of buildings, from the 1920s and 1930s, especially Sumner Spaulding's Frary Hall (1929).

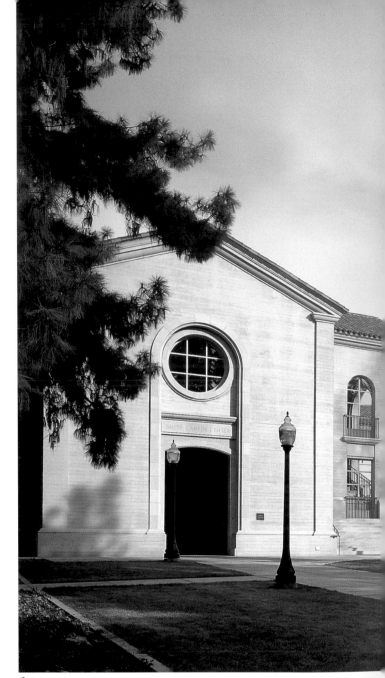

2

1

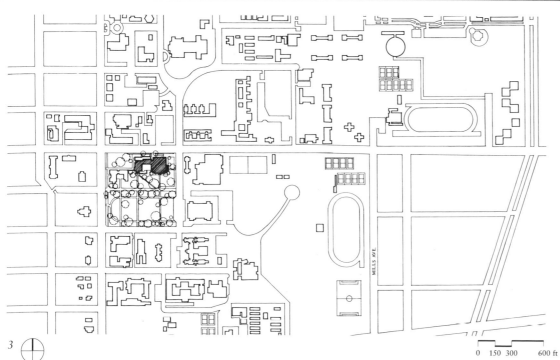

MILLS AVE.

0   150 300   600 ft

4. *East entrance to open-air gallery*
5. *View from southwest toward Mount Baldy*

Overleaf
6. *West entrance to open-air gallery*
7. *Double-height open-air gallery looking west*

4

5

8. Open-air stair hall
9. Courtyard with
   Reba Taylor Stover
   Memorial Fountain

8

9

10. *Second-floor plan*
11. *Ground-floor plan*
12. *Basement plan*
13. *Harry and Grace Steele Forum*

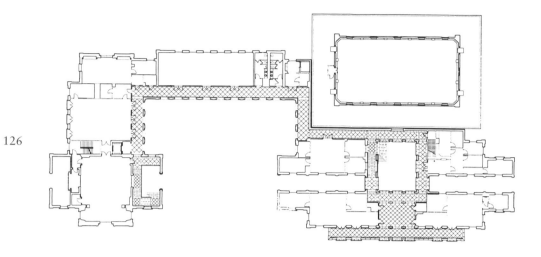

10

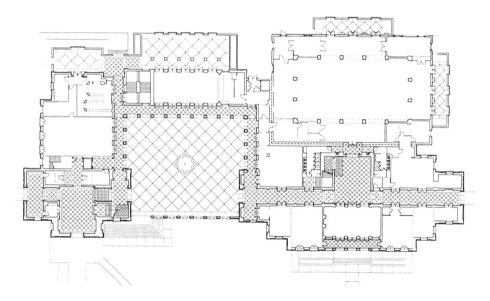

11

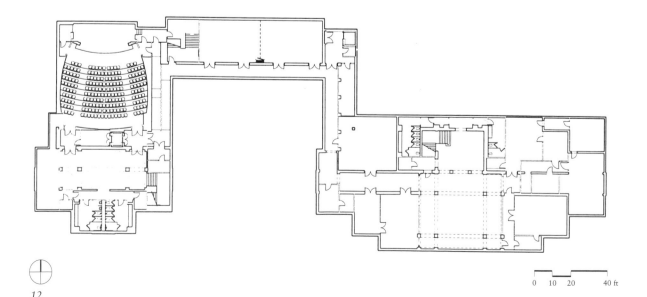

0   10   20   40 ft

12

14. *Rose Hills Theatre*
15. *Kinsmith Fountain*
    restaurant
16. *Gilbert Lounge*

14

15

17. *Hart Terrace from northeast*
18. *Reba Taylor Stover Memorial Fountain*

17

18

National Advocacy Center

Columbia, South Carolina
1993–1998

132 The National Advocacy Center, built on the campus of the University of South Carolina, combines guestrooms, classrooms, and offices in a 262,000-square-foot building dedicated to the training of federal legal personnel. The center also includes facilities for training district attorneys under the auspices of the National District Attorneys' Association.

At the heart of the center's design are ten identical high-technology courtrooms carefully planned to accommodate the specific training requirements of district-court, appellate-court, and grand-jury formats. Mock trials enacted within these training courtrooms are recorded for viewing by small groups of students and their advocacy coaches in any of twenty playback rooms. Computerized, video-capable lecture halls with tiered floors and horseshoe seating foster the center's Socratic instructional method.

Trainees are housed in 264 residence rooms and may dine in the south-facing, ground-floor, double-height dining room or in a less formal pub two floors above.

1. *Ground-floor plan*
2. *Main entrance from south*

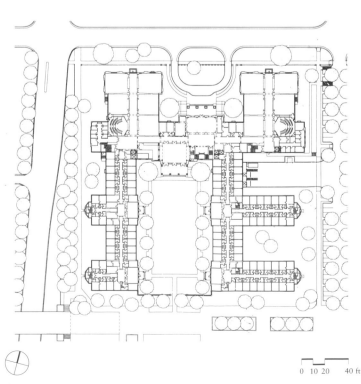

0 10 20   40 ft

1

2

3

4

Kitchenette-equipped breakout rooms are located within the center's two residential wings, providing space for informal meetings and group study.

The siting, massing, and architectural expression of the National Advocacy Center look to the three- and four-story brick, stone, and stucco buildings of the historic core of the University of South Carolina. It thus distinguishes itself from the austere concrete academic buildings built in the 1960s that abut the site on the south and east, and connects with the architecture surrounding the university's historic early-nineteenth-century lawn, the so-called Horseshoe, the design of which is attributed to Robert Mills.

6. *Main lobby*
   chandelier
7. *Main lobby*

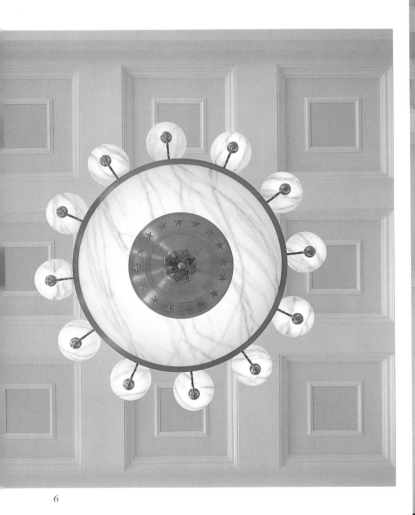

6

7

8. *Detail at main
   stair*
9. *Main stair from
   lobby*

10

11

Residence in Pacific Heights

San Francisco, California
1994–1999

144 Strict zoning and zealously protected view corridors played a dramatic role in shaping this design, fostering an architecture that outside of San Francisco might seem idiosyncratic but here is distinctly site-specific. As with our Russian Hill house (1989), this residence draws upon the work of distinguished architects who in the early 1900s helped stamp San Francisco's residential neighborhoods with a particular version of the architectural character of East Coast suburbs: Ernest Coxhead, Willis Polk, and Bernard Maybeck.

The shingle-clad house confronts the street with a two-and-a-half-story asymmetrical mass culminating in a lantern that bathes the generous central hall in soft light. At the rear, where the steeply sloping site allowed the insertion of an additional floor, a flat, symmetrically organized facade is relieved by an overscaled bay window that permits sweeping views across the Marina District to San Francisco Bay.

1. Site plan
2. Street facade
3. Front court
4. Garden facade

2

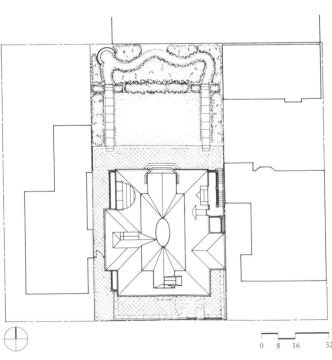

0   8   16   32 ft

1

3

4

5. *Stair hall looking west*
6. *Living room looking to dining room*

5

6

7. *Master bedroom looking north*
8. *First-floor plan*
9. *Second-floor plan*
10. *Library looking south*

7

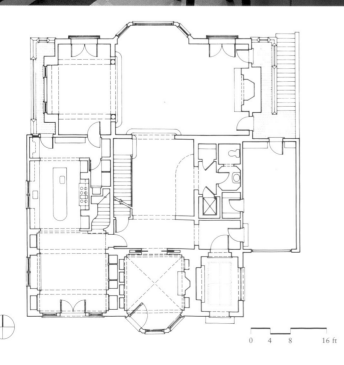

8

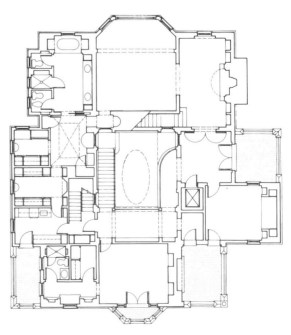

9

0 4 8   16 ft

11. *Stair hall*
    looking north
12. *Stair hall*

Robert C. Byrd United States Courthouse and Federal Building

Beckley, West Virginia
1994–1999

1. Site plan
2. East facade from Main Street

152 To allow the new federal complex planned for Beckley—a hundred-thousand-square-foot courthouse and a sixty-thousand-square-foot IRS office building, with a shared civic lobby—to serve as the centerpiece for the revitalization of the town's business district, the U.S. General Services Administration selected a central but ill-defined midblock site with challenging topography. Our design, winner of the first design excellence competition sponsored by the GSA, uses an open-air arcade to form a pedestrian route connecting the ceremonial entrance on Main Street and the more workaday entry on First Avenue. Court activities are located at the eastern portion of the site to ensure a strong civic presence on Main Street; the dignity of the law is

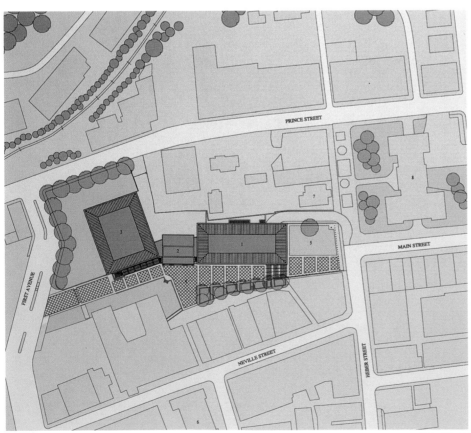

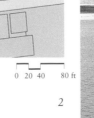

0 20 40   80 ft

1

2

154   proclaimed across a security buffer that is treated as a landscaped forecourt.

The building's principal materials—light tawny brick, limestone-colored precast stone, and gunmetal-gray metal roofs, windows, and panels—sit comfortably among the neighboring buildings. The three building components are of varying heights: four, three, and two stories. The courthouse, IRS block, and civic lobby help relate the scale of the complex to that of the adjacent county courthouse and existing federal buildings. All three parts of the complex, as well as the arcade, overlook a midblock landscaped passageway that helps knit the new federal complex into the fabric of downtown Beckley.

4

4. *Civic lobby loggia from south plaza*
5. *Arcade connecting Main Street to civic lobby loggia*
6. *Stair from south plaza to loggia looking northeast*
7. *Stair from south plaza to loggia looking west*

5

6

7

158

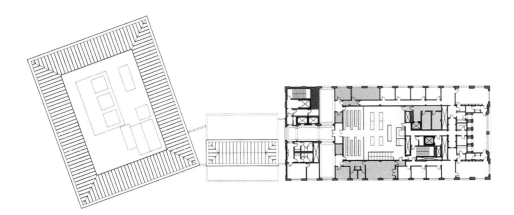

8

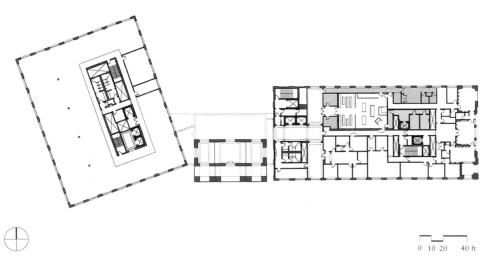

9

0 10 20   40 ft

11. *District chambers library*
12. *District courtroom*

11

12

Residence and Guest House

Southampton, New York
1994–1997

162   This main house, guest house, swimming pool, and tennis court are situated on a former field in a way that maximizes its potential as a landscape of broad lawns and trees. The symmetrical composition of the gambrel-roofed principal mass of the main house, reflecting the local Colonial Georgian vernacular, is set off by asymmetrical flanking wings, suggesting dependent cottages, that help reduce the scale. To the south, a one-and-a-half-story library pavilion, linked to the main section of the house by a book-lined gallery, shares a small private garden with the screened-in porch. To the north, the kitchen and family room are sheltered under a gabled roof that sweeps down to the eave of a one-story porch that extends along the entire north wall of the house. The more informally massed guest house, incorporating a squash court, combines both hipped and gabled forms and repeats details from the main house.

1

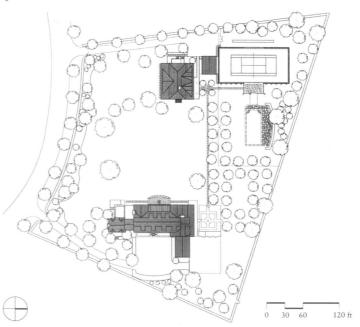

0   30 60   120 ft

2

1. West facade
2. Site plan

3. Detail at entry
4. View from
   southwest

3

4

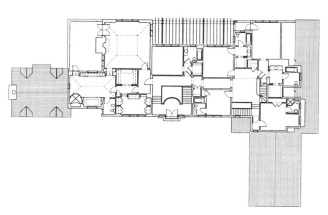

5, 6

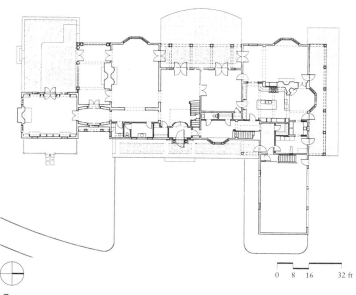

7

0   8   16   32 ft

5. Living room
6. Second-floor plan
7. First-floor plan

8

9

11. Family room
12. Library
13. Book gallery
    looking to
    library

11

12

14. Guest house
15. View past guest
    house to main
    house

14

15

16

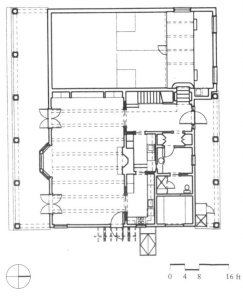

0 4 8   16 ft

17

18

Tribeca Park

400 Chambers Street
Battery Park City,
New York, New York
1995–1999

176　Various setbacks, each responding
to the scale of adjoining streets and to
the heights and daylight requirements
of present and future neighbors, break
down the apparent mass of this 453,000-
square-foot, 27-story building, which
contains 396 rental apartments. In
response to guidelines established by the
Battery Park City Authority's master plan,
a continuous curving street wall, recalling
Riverside Drive on New York's Upper
West Side, overlooks Governor Nelson A.
Rockefeller Park. The apartments
surround two sides of a secure south-
facing landscaped garden; a glazed
pavilion on the third side houses an
indoor swimming pool. To present a
grittier, more "downtown" image than
hitherto typical of Battery Park City's
apartment houses, massing and details,
such as a metal cornice and an exposed
wooden water tower on the roof,
deliberately recall characteristic features
of buildings in nearby Tribeca.

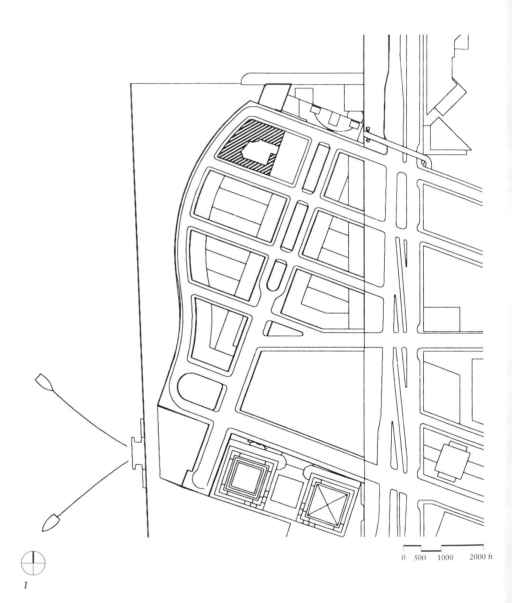

0　500　1000　　2000 ft

1

3

4

5. *View from northwest*
6. *Chambers Street*
   with main entrance
7. *Main entrance*

6

7

8

8. Elevator vestibule
9. Ground-floor plan
10. Concierge desk
11. Plan of floors four
   through nine

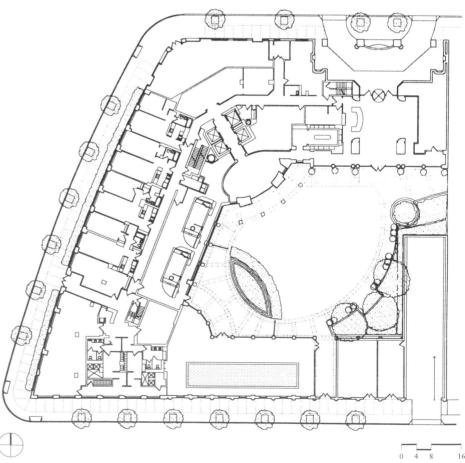

0 4 8   16 ft

9

10

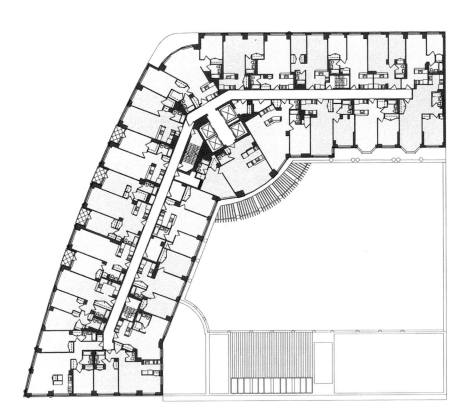

11

Edison Field

Anaheim, California
1995–1998

1

Edison Field began life in 1966 as a precast-concrete baseball stadium. In 1980, a major renovation to accommodate football encircled the field with a steel superstructure. Our task was to strip away the 1980 additions and transform the original into a venue that would convey in a modern way the spirit of a traditional ballpark.

At the entrance plaza, two baseball-cap-shaded structures and a bat-supported marquee dramatize the sense of arrival and event. Landscaped areas, including a playful food-concession area designed by Disney Imagineering, separate the ball field from the vast parking lots, providing a pleasant setting that encourages fans to arrive early and to linger after the game. The new design features of the stadium have drawn more fans, and their added enthusiasm has improved the Angels' performance: the team won its first World Series in 2002.

1. *Main entrance plaza at Home Plate Building*
2. *Canopy at entrance*
3. *Shade structure at entrance plaza*

2

3

188

4

4. *Aerial view*
5. *Field-level plan*
6. *Restaurants at stadium apron*

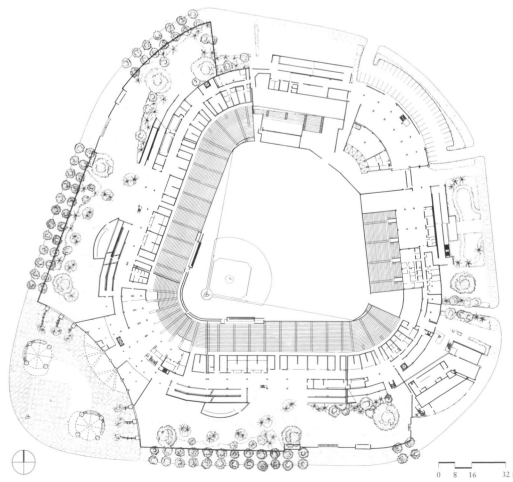

0 8 16   32 ft

5

7. Main entrance
8. Playing field

7

8

9. Field-level promenade
10. Private club lounge
11. Club-level restaurant at stadium apron

9

10

Residence

Kiawah Island, South Carolina
1995–2003

194 Inspired by the rustic shingled cottages designed by McKim, Mead & White for the Montauk Association on Long Island, the relatively simple, scaled-down rectangular mass and gabled roof of this house are softened by secondary gables and dormers, bay windows, and at the main floor, a broad wraparound porch. Flood conditions on Kiawah Island require that habitable spaces be set a full story above grade; here a battered and shingled foundation wall forms a plinth for the Tuscan colonnade of the porch. On the entry facade, a brick chimney bisects the center gable, providing a strong vertical counterpoint to the equally strong horizontal base.

Inside, the principal rooms are arranged en suite along the ocean side; rhythmically disposed, deeply angled bays offer views from each room to the east and west, both along the shoreline and out to sea. A similar arrangement is employed for the bedrooms on the second level; on the third floor, a home office reached by a hidden stair is a private aerie occupying the center of the house.

1

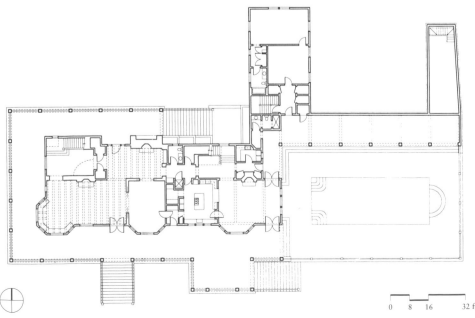

0   8   16   32 ft

2

1. South (beachfront)
   facade
2. First-floor plan
3. Pool deck

3

4. *North (entry) facade under construction*
5. *South (beachfront) facade under construction*
6. *Site plan*
7. *South facade from beach*

196

4

5

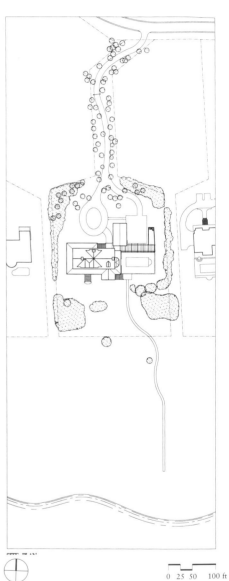

6

0 25 50   100 ft

Disney Ambassador Hotel
Tokyo Disney Resort

Urayasu-shi, Chiba-ken, Japan
1996–2000

198 Part of a new shopping and entertainment district at the gateway to the Tokyo Disney Resort, which comprises Tokyo Disneyland and DisneySea, the Ambassador, the first Disney-branded hotel in Japan, looks back to the moderne architecture of the 1930s, a style that exemplified an era when travel and movies offered the promise of glamour and romantic escape. The hotel contains five hundred guest rooms, facilities for fairy-tale weddings and banquets, and four restaurants designed by Marty Dorf Associates. To prevent visual intrusion into the adjacent theme parks, the building is organized around two courtyards that offer real-life versions of the elaborate sets of 1930s movie musicals: one is a formal garden entered from the lobby lounge; the other, a glamorous swimming pool court.

1

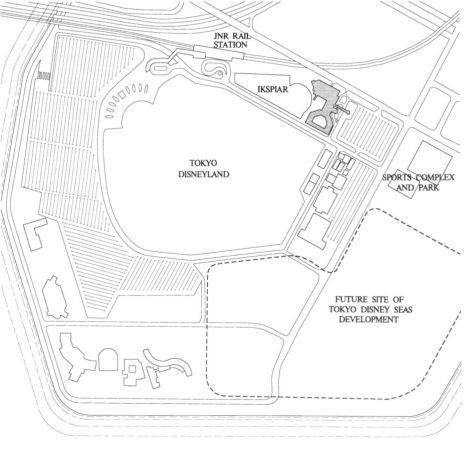

2

0   125   250 m

4

5

6

9

10

12. Pool detail
13. Fountain at pool
14. Pool court

12

13

14

15. Alcove at lobby lounge
16. Ground-floor plan
17. Lobby

15

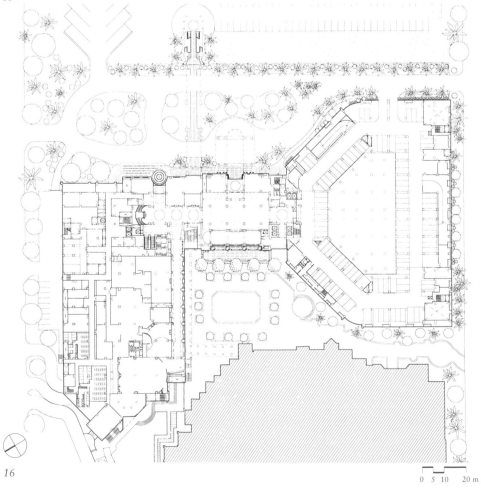

16

0 5 10 20 m

18. *Grand stair*
19. *Passage to*
    grand stair

18

19

20

21

24. Health club entrance
25. Guest room entrances
26. Guest room corridor

24, 25

27. *Detail of restaurant
    gallery*
28. *Restaurant gallery*

27

28

29

30

Residential Quadrangle and Leo J. O'Donovan Central Dining Facility Georgetown University

Washington, D.C.
1996–2003

1. *Model from southwest*
2. *Site plan*
3. *View from southwest*
4. *View from west*

224 This group of projects—780-student residential quadrangle, 1,200-seat dining hall, 800-car underground parking garage, and bus maintenance facility—represents the first component of our master plan for Georgetown University's 102-acre campus. Along with a new residence hall for Georgetown's Jesuit community (designed by another architect), the residence and O'Donovan Hall, the dining facility, surround a half-acre plaza that forms a new entrance to the university and opens to views of the Potomac River to the south.

The residential quadrangle consists of three interconnected six- to eight-story residence halls. The upper floors are organized as "neighborhoods" for not more than forty-two students each. The ground floor of the residence halls, which incorporates a mail room, library, and recreation, meeting, and music practice rooms as well as five faculty apartments, is penetrated by a vaulted open-air gallery that connects the new quadrangle to playing fields and future buildings to the north. At the southeast corner of the quadrangle, O'Donovan Hall comprises two 580-seat dining halls and a 40-seat private dining room with associated serving kitchens. Both the residence halls and the dining facility are clad in red brick with buff-colored cast-stone trim and dark gray slate roofs to reflect Georgetown's traditional architecture, especially Healy Hall, the university's signature building.

1

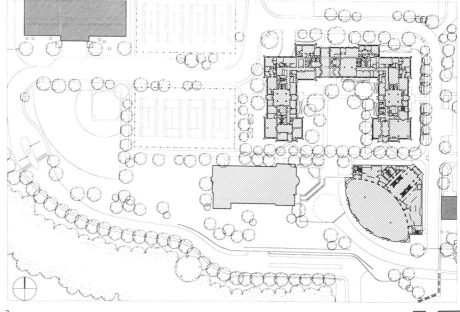

2

0 25 50   100 ft

3

4

5

5. *Dining hall study model*
6. *Residence hall ground-floor plan*
7. *Dining hall ground-floor plan*

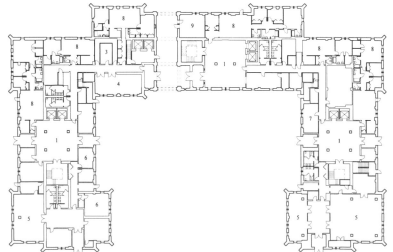

6

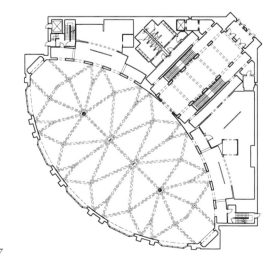

7

Highlands Village

Aspen, Colorado
1996–2002

1. *Site plan*
2. *View from south*

228   For decades, Aspen Highlands was Colorado's diamond in the rough. In spite of some of the best expert ski terrain in North America and the greatest vertical drop of any ski area in Colorado, inadequate lifts, long lines, and a virtually undeveloped base area compromised the mountain's appeal. New owners have opened ski trails and lifts, improved terrain, and developed a village at the base of the mountain consisting of a lodge, shops, restaurants, apartments, and a sophisticated hotel lining a sun-drenched pedestrian street and south-facing plaza. Flanking the village, two residential neighborhoods contain single-family houses and townhouses, most with direct access to the slopes. Parking for the village is located in a 670-car, two-level underground parking lot. The architecture of Highlands Village, with its native stone, logs, and rough clapboards, draws inspiration from such distinctly American precedents as the Ahwahnee Inn in Yosemite National Park, Old Faithful Lodge in Yellowstone Park, Timberline Lodge on Mount Hood, and Paradise Lodge on Mount Rainier to reaffirm an "American alpine" tradition.

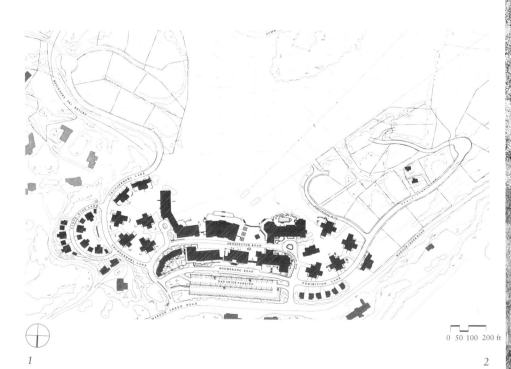

0 50 100 200 ft

1

2

3. *Elkhorn Lodge*
   porte cochere
4. *Elkhorn Lodge*
   south facade and
   pool terrace

230

3

4

5. South facade of
   village facing ski
   slopes
6. Facade detail
   at Maroon Creek
   Road

5, 6

Federal Reserve Bank of Atlanta

Atlanta, Georgia
1996–2001

236   The Federal Reserve Bank of Atlanta, which houses the Sixth Federal Reserve District Headquarters and the Atlanta branch, occupies an important site on the west side of Peachtree Street, between Tenth and Eleventh Streets. The 750,000-square-foot building combines a ten-story office tower, a low base housing a conference center, and facilities for processing checks and cash. The goals for the project were to create a facility that would satisfy the bank's functional requirements for the next twenty-five years, to contribute to the redevelopment of Midtown Atlanta, and to present an image of the stability of a model public institution.

Drawing on the Sixth Federal Reserve District's own architectural history, and on Paul Cret's Federal Reserve headquarters in Washington (1935), the white marble Atlanta Fed is classical in a modern way. The paired, oversized windows of the forty-two-thousand-square-foot typical floors are laid out on a module appropriate to the Fed's specific planning needs. The paved plaza and park facing Peachtree Street, as well as other landscaped areas, act as security buffers while providing the general public with accessible open space. Most staff and many visitors arrive either by MARTA, Atlanta's subway system, or by car and enter through a third-floor lobby, which serves a five-hundred-space parking garage at the building's west end and connects to Tenth Street Station; other visitors, including large numbers of schoolchildren, enter through the double-height main lobby—a grand Georgia-quarried-marble room detailed with stainless steel—to visit the money museum, view an orientation film, and tour the facility.

1

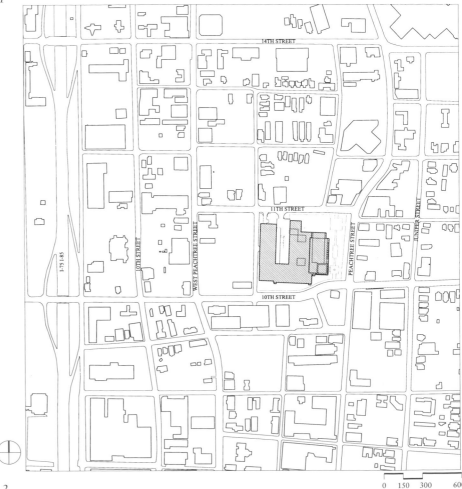

2

4. *View from west*
5. *View from Tenth Street*
6. *Peachtree Street facade*

4

5

7. Third-level (west) building entrance
8. Facade detail with historic column from original Federal Reserve Bank of Atlanta (A. Ten Eyck Brown, 1918)

7, 8

9

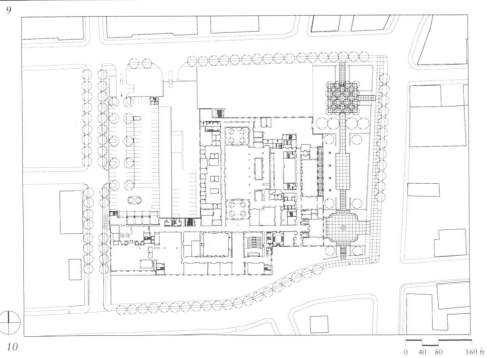

10

0   40   80   160 ft

Heavenly View Ranch

Snowmass, Colorado
1996–1999

246 At an elevation of 8,700 feet, this house enjoys the highest, and perhaps most remote, site we have encountered. To provide comfortable accommodations for three generations of a close-knit family, the lodgelike house employs a rustic vocabulary of logs, timbers, and rough-hewn stone to form a low-lying composition of linked pavilions wrapping the brow of the hill. A vaulted living room under a spreading gable roof is complemented by a towerlike family room, the only vertical element to rise above the shed-roofed wings that contain the master suite, kitchen, and service areas.

1. *View from*
   southwest

1

2. *View from first-floor deck*
3. *First-floor plan*
4. *South facade*

2

0 4 8   16 ft

5, 6

Diagonal Mar Entertainment and Retail Center

Barcelona, Spain
1996–2001

254   This 1.2-million-square-foot, three-story urban entertainment and retail center, part of an eighty-four-acre development that also includes 2.2 million square feet of medium- and high-rise apartment buildings, eight hundred thousand square feet of hotels and offices, and a thirty-four-acre public park, occupies an important site at the seaside terminus of the recently extended Avenida Diagonal, at the eastern edge of Barcelona's Eixample street grid, which was established by Ildefons Cerdà in 1859. Our design recasts the typical inward-looking exurban American model for the urban European setting. Glazed store-fronts and shop windows face out to the sidewalks wherever possible. Provision for a future metro stop supplements five thousand below-grade parking spaces. On the top floor, restaurants open onto a wide plaza that faces the sea.

1

2

0 25 50   100 m

3

0 50 100   200 m

Hobby Center
for the Performing Arts

Houston, Texas
1996–2002

1. Main entrance canopy
2. Site plan
3. Entry facade looking
   north along Bagby
   Street
4. View from Tranquility
   Park

256   The Hobby Center for the Performing Arts is a 270,000-square-foot performing-arts complex consisting of the 2,650-seat Sarofim Hall, the 500-seat Zilkha theater, and the Humphreys School of Musical Theater. The site is bounded by a bayou and elevated freeways to the west, by Houston's theater district to the north, and by high-rise office buildings to the east, across Tranquility Park, which form the backdrop to the 70-foot-high grand lobby. Separate public entrances are provided for the restaurant, community theater, and school.

The complex is broken up into distinct volumes representing the major program elements. Each of the volumes has a distinctive shape; the composition, seen from above, culminates in a skylight above the grand lobby. A covered galleria connects the main entrance plaza with an eight-hundred-car garage along Buffalo Bayou.

The major building materials are limestone, brick, painted steel columns, glazed curtain wall, and standing-seam metal roofing. Public art is an important component of the design: a large mural by Sol LeWitt forms the north wall of the grand lobby and a bronze sculpture by Anthony Cragg stands on the plaza.

1

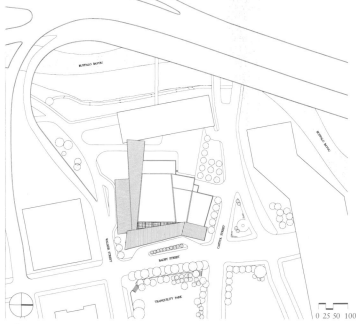

2

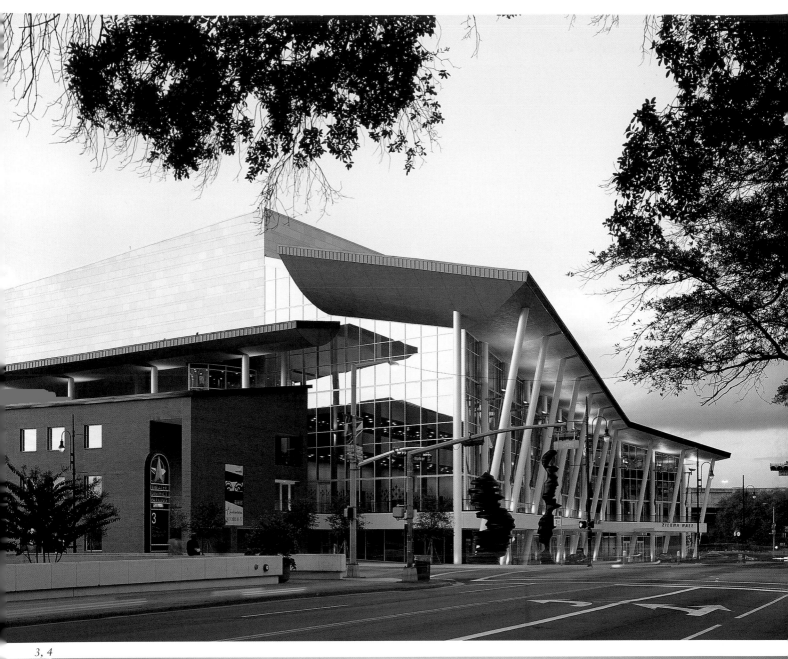

3, 4

5. *Galleria*
6. *Stair from ticket
   lobby to grand lobby*
7. *Galleria*

5, 6

8. *Ticket lobby*
9. *Ground-floor plan*
10. *Main-floor plan*
11. *Grand lobby*

260

8

9

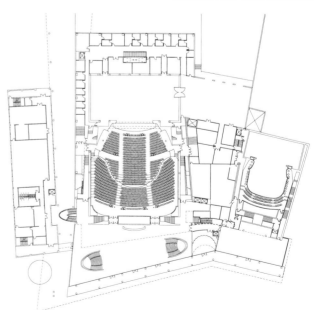

0 12 24   48 ft

10

12. *Sarofim Hall*
    looking south
13. *Sarofim Hall*
    looking east

14. *Zilkha Hall
    looking north*
15. *Zilkha Hall
    looking east*

14

15

16. *View from Tranquility Park*
17. *View south along Bagby Street*

Overleaf
18. *View from Tranquility Park with City Hall (left)*

16, 17

Guest House and Tennis Pavilion

Brentwood, California
1996–1999

270   When clients for whom we had designed
a summer house on the East Coast moved
west, they asked us to complement their
forty-year-old Wallace Neff–designed
Country French house with a new guest
house. A screening room occupies most
of the hipped-roof, timber-trimmed,
partially whitewashed brick outbuilding;
a corner turret houses the entry and
a guest bedroom above.

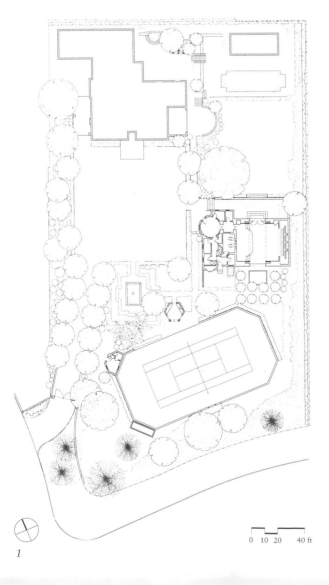

2

1. *Site plan*
2. *Guest house entry*
3. *Entry facade of main
   house (Wallace Neff,
   1968)*

0 10 20   40 ft

1

4. North facade
   of guest house
5. View from guest
   house toward
   tennis court
6. Tennis court and
   pavilion looking
   toward guest
   house

4

5

7

Street Furniture for J. C. Decaux

1996–

276   Advertising company J. C. Decaux commissioned designs for a coherent collection of street furniture—bus shelters, newsstands, public toilets, vending kiosks, and so on—as part of an effort to obtain franchises in return for income generated by the advertising carried on the structures. Our solutions are unified by a kit of interchangeable parts inspired by the industrial classicism of street furniture from the early twentieth century, such as New York's old IRT subway entrances and the Chicago El. The city of Chicago recently selected our designs for a major street-furniture initiative.

1

2

1. Bus shelter
2. Computer model
   of traffic controller's
   booth
3. Rendering of vend-
   ing pavilion

3

Broadway Residence Hall
Columbia University and
Morningside Heights Branch
New York Public Library

New York, New York
1996–2000

1. *South facade*
2. *View along Broadway from West 116th Street*
3. *View from southwest*

278 Located at the northeast corner of West 113th Street and Broadway, on the edge of Columbia's historic McKim, Mead & White campus, the fourteen-story, 371-bed Broadway Residence Hall faces away from the campus and toward the city on the south and west. The undergraduate dormitory is entered from West 114th Street, across from Alfred Lerner Hall, Columbia's recently rebuilt student center. The entrance also serves Hogan Hall, a former retirement home that was converted to a student residence in the 1970s. The wood-paneled lobby and the lounge on the ground level reflect the character of similar elements on the campus. A coffee area was created in what was once the courtyard of Hogan Hall.

The building, which incorporates the facade of a five-story red-brick townhouse designed by George Keister in 1905, is clad in cast-stone-trimmed tawny brick, which was selected after extensive discussion with both the university and members of the surrounding Morningside Heights community, who preferred a design in the spirit of the residential apartment buildings that line Broadway rather than one that matched the red brick and limestone of the Columbia campus.

The two lower floors of the building are largely devoted to retail and to the seventeen-thousand-square-foot Morning-side Heights branch of the New York Public Library. The library interior was inspired by the restrained classicism of early-twentieth-century Carnegie branches, with paneled columns and ceiling beams, decorative metal railings, built-in wood bookshelves, and a slate floor in the entrance lobby. Above, the building forms a south-facing U, with bedrooms in the east and west wings and a communal kitchen and lounge at the center of each floor. A penthouse contains two large study lounges with fine city views.

1

2

6. Lounge at penthouse
7. Typical residential-
floor plan
8. Entry lounge

6

0   5   10 ft

7

9

9. Reading room,
   Morningside
   Heights Branch
10. Reference desk
11. Circulation desk
12. Second-floor plan
13. First-floor plan
14. Library entrance
    on Broadway

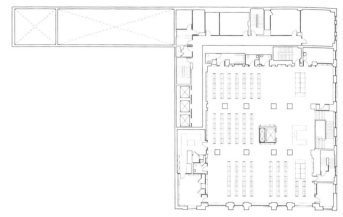

12

10

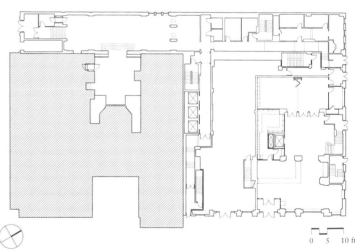

13

0   5   10 ft

11

Edgewater Apartments

*West Vancouver,
British Columbia, Canada
1997–2000*

1

Containing fifteen luxury units—three
townhouse apartments at the base, eleven
full-floor tower apartments, and a two-
story penthouse—and massed in response
to strict setback and height restrictions,
this tower capitalizes on views of English
Bay to the south and west and West
Vancouver's uplands to the north. The
pedimented vault at the roof creates
dramatic interior spaces in the penthouse
apartment and simultaneously masks
mechanical functions that would
otherwise disturb neighbors on the nearby
hillside. The bold top and the carefully
considered entry court distinguish the
building from its unimaginative high-rise
neighbors.

1. *View from English Bay*
2. *Site plan with garden-
   level and lobby-level
   plans*

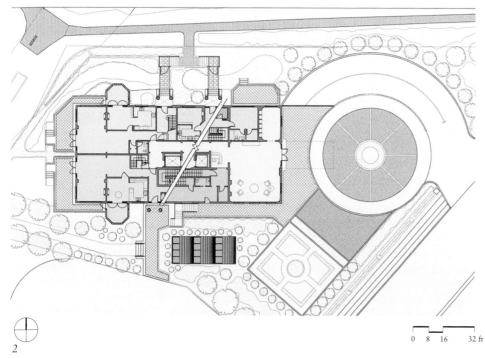

0   8   16   32 ft

3

4

6. *View from English*
   Bay
7. *View from uplands*

6, 7

8

9

10

8. *View to English Bay from typical apartment*
9. *Lobby*
10. *Plan of floors two through eleven*
11. *Swimming pool*

0 4 8   16 ft

Rodgers Recreation Center
Salve Regina University

Newport, Rhode Island
1997–2000

1. Aerial view from east
2. First-floor plan
3. View of entrance porch through arched breezeway of Hennery (Peabody & Stearns, 1885)

294 Salve Regina University is located in the heart of Newport's famous "summer cottage" district. The school does not have a distinct campus but is instead scattered throughout the neighborhood in a handful of undistinguished, purpose-built structures amid its extensive holdings of historic houses, including H. H. Richardson's Watts-Sherman House (1874–1875) and Richard Morris Hunt's Ochre Court (1880–1881), as well as minor gems like Peabody & Stearns's Hennery. Our design returns to the Shingle-style architecture that is a vital part of Newport's heritage, as exemplified by McKim, Mead & White's Casino (1879–1880).

The Rodgers Recreation Center provides Salve Regina with much-needed athletic facilities, including two basketball courts in a clear-span gymnasium, weight-training room, aerobics studio, administrative offices, conference room, and hall-of-fame gallery. The lobby and entrance porch are generously scaled to serve as campus gathering places. The building occupies the center of a large site at the end of an axial walkway leading from Ochre Court, now the university's main administrative building. To keep the open character of the site and minimize the apparent mass of the building, more than half of its square footage is below grade. Columned porches wrap the facility, which is largely windowless both to provide privacy in the various training rooms and to reduce the impact of its bright interior lighting on residential neighbors.

1

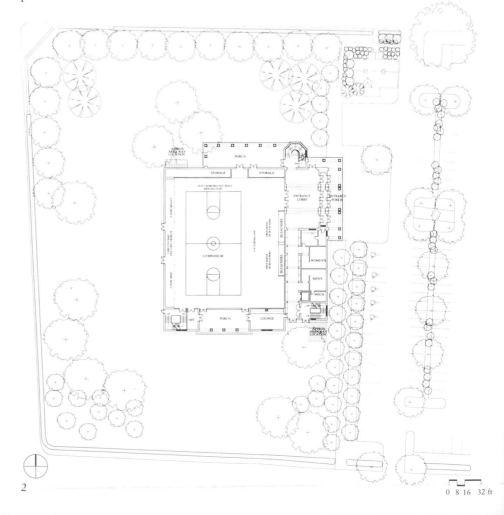

2

0 8 16   32 ft

4

5

4. South porch
5. Roof dormer detail
6. West facade
7. Main entrance from
   northeast

6

8. Reception desk and
   trophy gallery
9. Lower-level plan
10. Gymnasium

8

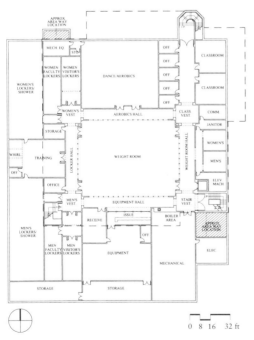

9

10

Knott Science Center Addition College of Notre Dame of Maryland

Baltimore, Maryland
1997–2000

300   The campus of the College of Notre Dame of Maryland, North America's oldest Catholic women's college, enjoys a spacious hilltop site in the northern suburbs of Baltimore. Challenged by the competition for students and by the need to strengthen its programs and facilities, especially in the sciences, the college commissioned us to develop a master plan to help guide its growth in the twenty-first century. The plan reorganizes roads, playing fields, parking, and pedestrian paths and proposes a number of new buildings and additions. The first of these is the addition to the Knott Science Center, a forty-thousand-square-foot, four-story wing providing state-of-the-art laboratories, support space, classrooms, and offices, as well as a dignified entrance to what was, at best, a workhorse building from 1961. Stylistically, the new wing refers to the Gothic of Gibbons Hall (1873), the college's first building and still its most important.

1. View from northeast
2. Ground-floor plan
3. Entrance facade from west

1

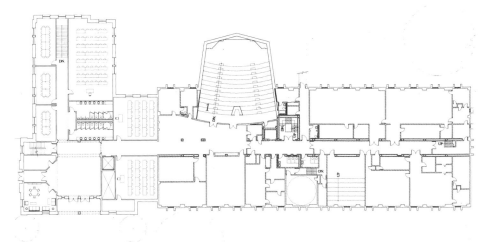

2

0 8 16   32 ft

4. Lobby
5. Corridor
6. Chemistry teaching
   laboratory

4

5

6

7

8

Manzanita Hall
College of Arts, Media, and Communication
California State University, Northridge

Northridge, California
1997–2001

1. Site plan
2. View of main
   entry from east

306 Part of a larger effort not only to rebuild the forty-three-year-old Northridge campus after the devastating earthquake of 1994 but also to give it a stronger architectural identity, Manzanita Hall, housing the College of Arts, Media, and Communication, includes offices, classrooms, television studios, and editing suites for three departments—journalism; communication studies; and radio, television, and film—as well as two galleries, a 120-seat screening room, and a 120-seat lecture hall.

A double-height glass-walled gallery atop a randomly fenestrated concrete-block base is capped by an upward curving metal roof carried on a colonnade of metal columns bundled in threes to complement the superscale of Oviatt Library, its partner across Sierra Quad. At the northeast corner of the building, the last bay of the colonnade shelters a triple-height entrance plaza, bounded to the south by a smooth-finished concrete wall that encloses the screening room. On the side of the building away from Sierra Quad, a simple stucco-clad L-shaped mass stretches west and south to form its own landscaped quadrangle.

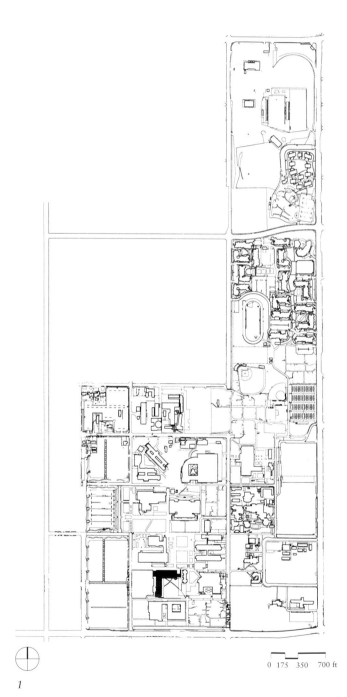

0 175 350   700 ft

1

3

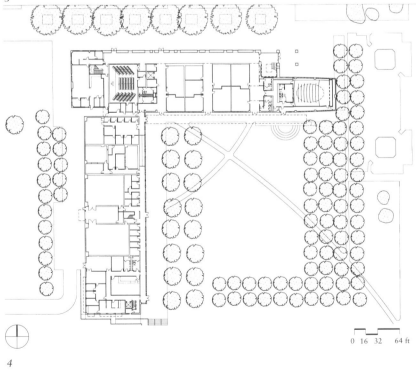

0 16 32   64 ft

4

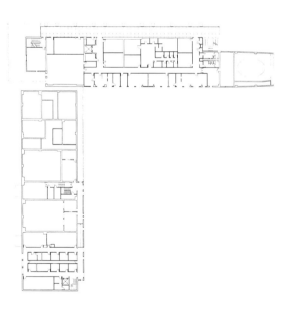

5

6

3. *View from south*
4. *Ground-floor plan*
5. *Second-floor plan*
6. *Covered arcade*

7

7. Detail at entry
8. View from northeast

8

9. *Entry hall*
10. *Grand stair and*
    upper hall
11. *Upper hall*

9

10

12. Screening room
13. Classroom
14. Detail at grand
    stair

12

13

15

Spangler Campus Center
Harvard Business School

Boston, Massachusetts
1997–2001

318　The design and construction of the Spangler Center occurred at a moment in the development of Harvard Business School when the school recognized that though it had been oriented only north to the historic campus of Harvard College across the Charles River in Cambridge, its future lay to the south toward Western Avenue and Boston, where its expansion and that of the university as a whole is likely to take place. While the Spangler Center currently marks an edge of the business school campus, one day it will be at its absolute center. Thus, the building opens not only to Aldrich Hall to the north, with which it forms a new court-yard that conforms with McKim, Mead & White's radial campus plan of 1927, but also to Western Avenue to the south across a landscaped courtyard. The elaborately pavilioned U-shaped structure ensures an abundance of natural light in all the public rooms. Multiple entrances enhance transparency from every direction. The design of the Spangler Center returns to McKim, Mead & White's planning principles and also to the formal language of the firm's buildings, an interpretation of Harvard's historic architecture of limestone-trimmed red brick, gray stucco, and slate.

Inside, double-height stair halls embrace three lounges that connect a 400-seat dining hall in the west wing and a large, divisible multipurpose room in the east. On the second floor, a suite of student-services offices is framed by two wings of group-study rooms; on the lower level are a grille, student mailboxes, case-study distribution center, campus store, copy center, post office, and 350-seat auditorium.

1

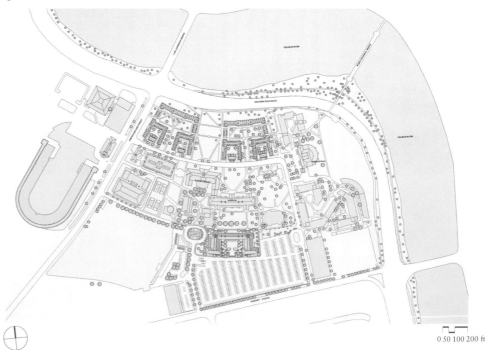

0 50 100 200 ft

2

1. *View from south*
2. *Campus plan*

320

3

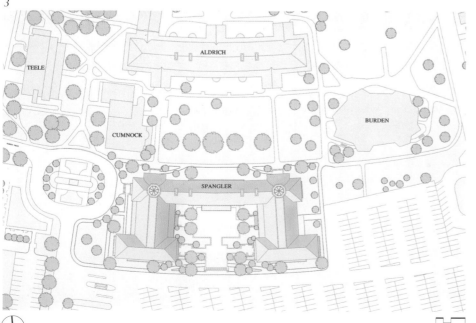

4

3. Aerial view from
south
4. Site plan
5. View from northeast
across Aldrich
Quadrangle

TEELE

ALDRICH

CUMNOCK

BURDEN

SPANGLER

0 20 40 80 ft

6

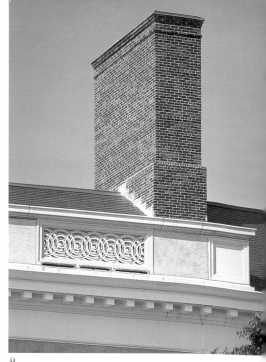

9

7, 8

SPANGLER

10, 11

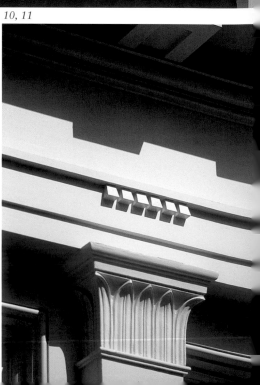

12, 13

14. Entrance rotunda
and stair hall
15. Second-floor plan
16. Ground-floor plan
17. Entrance rotunda
looking to lounges

14

15

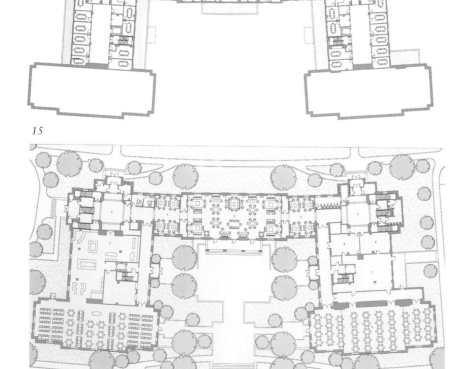

0 5 10 20 ft

16

18

19

21. Entrance to
    dining hall servery
22. Dining hall
    looking east

21

22

23. *Main lounge looking*
    to fireplace
24. *Main lounge*

23

24

25. *Student mailboxes*
26. *Student-services*
    center
27. *Grille*

25

26

The Chatham

181 East 65th Street
New York, New York
1997–2001

1. *View from southeast along Third Avenue*
2. *Ground-floor plan*
3. *Detail of upper floors*

334   This 231,000-square-foot condominium tower houses 94 apartments and 22,000 square feet of retail. Typical floors contain five apartments, while upper stories contain only one or two. Although the tower-on-base massing reflects New York's current zoning, the red-brick and limestone facades, articulated with French balconies, bay windows, and subtle changes in plane, recall luxury apartment buildings of the 1920s, such as those along Park Avenue. The top of the building consists of a series of setbacks and culminates in a lantern that identifies the building on the skyline.

1

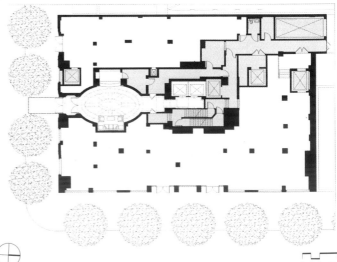

0 4 8 16 ft

2

4. *Third Avenue retail*
   facade
5. *Entrance*
6. *Skyline view across*
   Central Park

   Overleaf
7. *Lobby*

4

5

Apartment in the Chatham

New York, New York
1998–2001

1

My own apartment in the Chatham, situated on the west flank of the building, has views to a large private garden and, beyond, to the skyscrapers of midtown Manhattan. The design was inspired by Hollywood films of the 1930s and 1940s, which captured an idealized New York of glamour and modern sophistication. In this setting, the dialogue between a recollected and rearranged architectural past and contemporary art seems to work.

2

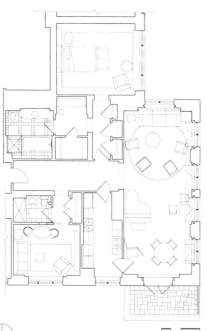

0 2 4   8 ft

3

5

6

344

7

8

The Seville

300 East 77th Street
New York, New York
1997–2002

1. Ground-floor plan
2. Typical upper-floor plan
3. View from northwest along Second Avenue

346 With its light-colored brick facade and black columnar brick accents, this 31-story, 170-unit apartment tower revisits New York's hotel and apartment buildings of the late 1920s and 1930s, when the emphasis on simple shapes and verticality, combined with corner windows and increased spans of glass, for the first time made the skyscraper typology suitable for urban living.

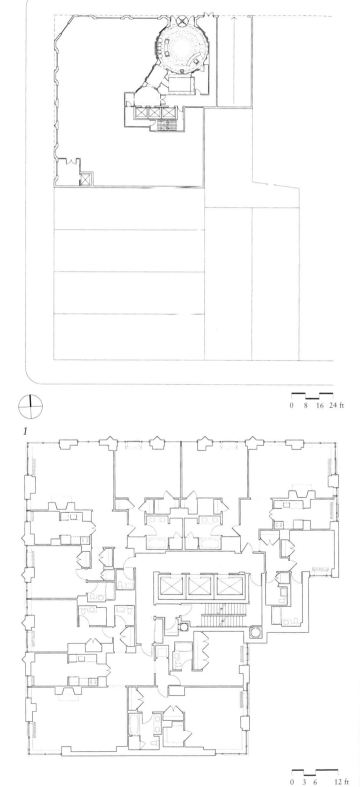

0 8 16 24 ft

1

2

0 3 6 12 ft

Aging and Allied Health Building and Gill Heart Institute
University of Kentucky Medical Center

Lexington, Kentucky
1998–2003

1. Entrance to Aging and Allied Health Building under construction
2. Site plan
3. Aging and Allied Health Building, gateway bridge, and Gill Heart Institute

348 Housing eleven of the College of Allied Health's departments, the office of the medical-center chancellor, and a ninety-bed geriatric inpatient nursing-care and teaching facility, the Aging and Allied Health Building is linked to the Gill Heart Institute by a bridge designed to create a new southern gateway to the university's Lexington campus. Boldly classical in style and executed in red brick, Indiana limestone, and matching cast stone, the designs build on the reduced Federal-style vocabulary of the historic campus core.

1

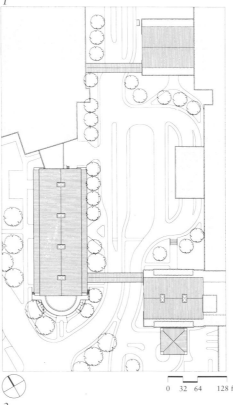

0 32 64   128 ft

2

3

Dream House for
This Old House Magazine

Wilton, Connecticut
1998–1999

350   *This Old House* magazine documented
the design and construction of this 5,500-
square-foot house. Placed on the northern
edge of a rolling site to permit panoramic
views from the major rooms and porch,
the house wraps around its entry courtyard; a series of connected volumes
diminishes its size while suggesting that
successive components were added slowly
and naturally over time.

1. Site plan
2. View from
   entry drive

0   25 50 ft

1

2

3. View from
   meadow
4. Porch

352

3

4

5. Stair hall
6. First-floor plan
7. Living room

5

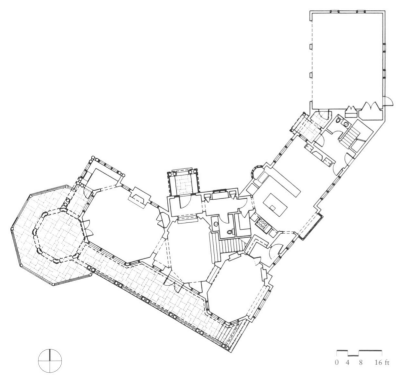

0 4 8 16 ft

6

Miami Beach Library
and Collins Park
Cultural Center

Miami Beach, Florida
1998–2003

356 The new Miami Beach Library epitomizes our commitment to place and tradition. The building recalls and reinforces the stylish yet relaxed modernism of Miami Beach architecture, capturing not only the clear shapes that work in the intense sunshine but also the shaded courtyards that provide welcome oases from busy streets and cloudless skies.

The forty-five-thousand-square-foot library serves as both a regional library and a community gathering place. The double-height lobby, with inverted tapering columns leading to a high band of clerestory windows, accommodates a gallery for community art shows. The ground floor contains a 140-seat auditorium, the general library collection, and a café that opens onto a walled garden with a fountain. The second floor includes a large children's library, a young-adult section overlooking the lobby, and a reading room for local history and special collections. The exterior is faced with Florida Keystone and stucco; a terra-cotta entablature faces Collins Park.

The creation of a new cultural campus surrounding Collins Park offers the opportunity to reinvent this strategically located space as a town square for Miami Beach, which currently has no proper civic gathering place or community green. Our plan, reestablishing the historic connection of Collins Park and the Bass Museum with the Atlantic Ocean, draws additional strength from the new library and the new home for the Miami City Ballet on its periphery. The park design includes the reuse of the auditorium of the existing 1960s library as a multi-purpose rotunda for the many local theater companies in Miami Beach; the remainder will be demolished. Meandering pathways reinterpret the historic design of Collins Park while providing a variety of different environments for sculpture, water pools, and passive recreation.

1

1. *Aerial view
   of library and
   Collins Park*
2. *Site plan*
3. *First-floor plan*

357

4

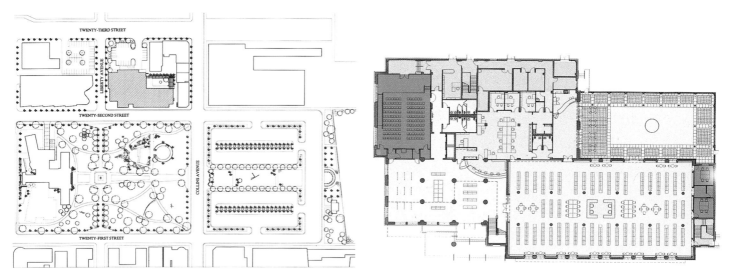

2

0 60 120 ft

3

0 5 10 20 ft

Torre del Ángel

Reforma 350
Mexico City, Mexico
1998–2000

358   Sometimes an architect's job is to make a silk purse out of a sow's ear. Our design for a nineteen-story office building on Mexico City's prestigious Paseo de la Reforma took a banal and clumsily detailed building of the early 1980s, stripped it to its structure, resculpted its mass, and reclad it in a sleek wall of glass.

While the existing building turned an aggressively serrated side face to a city landmark—the Angel of Mexican Independence Monument—Torre del Ángel instead presents a complementary backdrop of layered glass surfaces. The outermost layer, a gently scalloped glass curtain, rises from the street to an eighteenth-floor balcony, orienting the building toward the monument and announcing its relocated main entrance. Above street level, five floors of parking are ventilated through openings in a fritted-glass screen wall. An openwork metal cornice at the top of the building caps the facade while concealing window-washing equipment.

1. *Site plan*
2. *Facade detail*
3. *Existing building*
4. *View from base of Angel of Mexican Independence Monument (1910)*

2

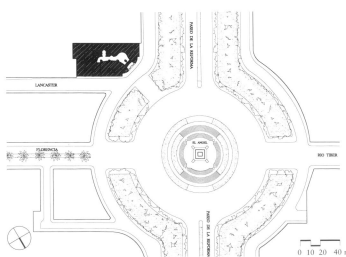

3

1

0 10 20   40 m

5. Ground-level
   elevator lobby
6. Ground-level
   plan
7. Lobby

Overleaf
8. View from north

5

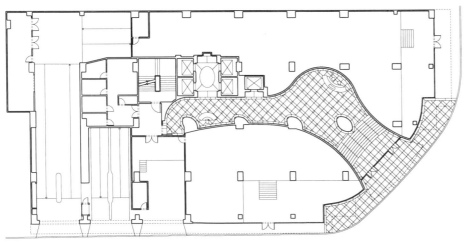

6

0 2 4   8 m

7

Nashville Public Library

Nashville, Tennessee
1998–2001

364   Nashville is "Music City, USA"; it is also the "Athens of the South," with a strong, distinct tradition of classicism that permeates its architecture, from such incomparable public buildings as William Strickland's Tennessee State Capitol to all strata of residential fabric. The commission for the central library, awarded to us

1

in a limited competition, represents our most complete and complex demonstration of modern classicism. The library's relationship with the capitol is made explicit not only in exterior massing and detailing but also in the organization of its plan, which takes advantage of a site on axis with the capitol's principal facade.

The library is both functional and grand; it is definitely not a supermarket for books. The 350,000-square-foot, three-story, buff-brick and Alabama-limestone building, with capacity for one million volumes, is fitted into a steeply sloping site, with portions of the upper two floors built atop an existing parking structure to look outward to the surrounding townscape and inward to a landscaped courtyard; the courtyard, with its central

1. *War Memorial (Edward E. Dougherty, 1925) and Tennessee State Capitol (William Strickland, 1845–1859) from library*
2. *Library from capitol steps*

2

366   fountain, pool, and covered arcade, provides an oasis and a setting for special readings and events.

The library's symbolic public areas—Ingram Hall; the Rascoe Bond Davis Nashville Room, which houses the local history collection; the gallery; the Memorial Foundation Grand Reading Room; the skylighted grand stair; and the Margaret Ann and Walter Robinson Courtyard—are all located on axis with the capitol. The main spaces are uniquely suited for social interaction, from the figural Grand Reading Room to the quiet eddies of informal seating that are distributed throughout the open stack areas, especially around the courtyard. The project involved an extraordinary amount of community input, including a public art program that enriched the building with work commissioned from local and national graphic artists, authors, photographers, painters, sculptors, and metalworkers.

4

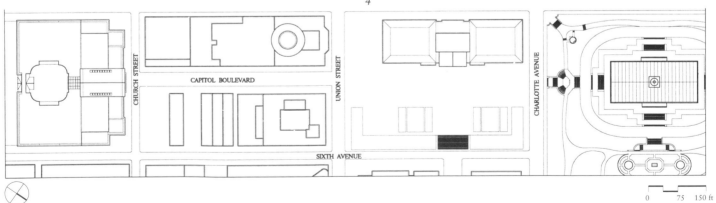

CHURCH STREET

CAPITOL BOULEVARD

UNION STREET

CHARLOTTE AVENUE

SIXTH AVENUE

0   75   150 ft

3

5

6

7. Courtyard loggia
8. Courtyard
   fountain detail
9. Courtyard

Overleaf
10. Lobby

7, 8

9

11. *Detail at upper stair hall*
12. *Stair hall*
13. *First-floor plan*
14. *Second-floor plan*

12

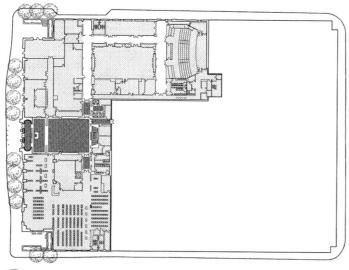

13

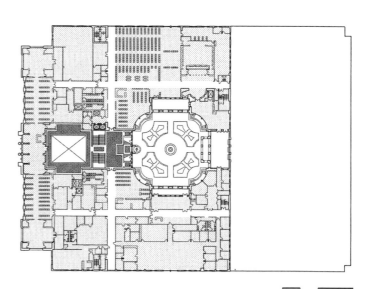

14

0   25   50   100 ft

15. *Upper stair hall
    looking to Grand
    Reading room*
16. *Detail of Richard
    Haas murals in
    upper stair hall*
17. *Upper stair
    hall looking
    to courtyard*

374

15

16

17

City of Nashville
1840

18. Nonfiction reading
    room
19. Arts-and-crafts
    room

18, 19

20

21

23. *Grand Reading Room*
24. *Detail at Grand Reading Room*

23, 24

25. Children's-services
   room
26. Entry to children's
   theater
27. Children's theater

25, 26

27

28

Peter Jay Sharp Boathouse

Swindler Cove Park, Upper Manhattan
New York, New York
1998–

386 Conceived and developed by the New York Restoration Project, a nonprofit organization that works to restore neglected landscapes to active public use, this boathouse is one element of a city and state plan to rehabilitate the Harlem River's blighted shoreline. The site, immediately to the south of Sherman Creek, was once home to many recreational boathouses, including those of Columbia and Fordham Universities, that in the late nineteenth and early twentieth centuries served a flourishing network of competitive rowing clubs.

To avoid harming the fragile intertidal environment, the painted board-and-batten, wood-framed boathouse has been designed as a floating structure, as were the earlier boathouses on the site. The facility will be entered from a promenade atop a nearby embankment via a gated entrance and a series of ramped fixed piers and floating docks. The first floor of the boathouse will contain storage space and a launching area for sixteen boats; administrative, exercise, and meeting rooms will be housed on the building's second floor, where spectators will be able to view crew practice and races from a generously proportioned deck sheltered by an expansive bracketed metal roof.

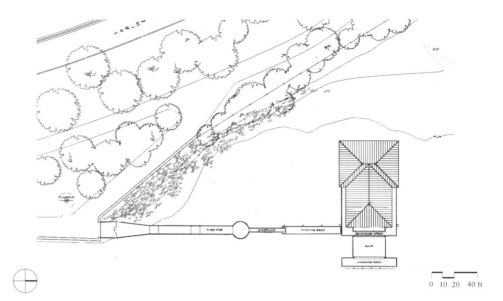

1

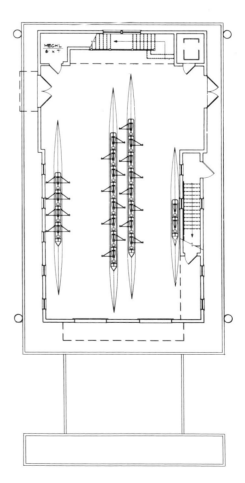

0 4 8   16 ft

2

1. *Site plan*
2. *First-floor plan*
3. *Model view from*
   northeast

3

Clearwater Public Library

Clearwater, Florida
2001–2003

388   Taking full advantage of a dramatic site on a bluff overlooking Coachman Park and the Intercoastal Waterway, this three-story, ninety-thousand-square-foot library will create a locally recognizable landmark that will help catalyze the redevelopment of the city's downtown. The building presents an urbane and dignified face to Osceola Avenue, reserving its more daring, exuberant expression for the park. The green space and the water are visible from a glass-enclosed staircase as well as from a café and reading rooms where large windows are shaded by an extension of the undulating roof that forms a superscale porch.

1. *View from southwest*
2. *Osceola Avenue*
   entrance
3. *Reading room*
4. *View from northwest*
5. *Site plan*
6. *Ground-floor plan*

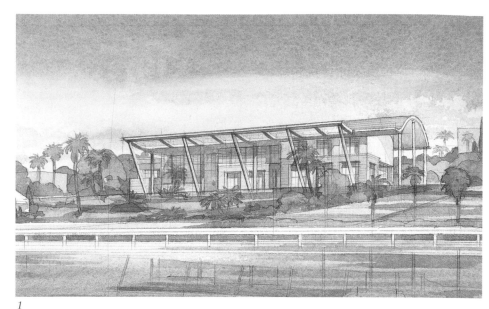

1

2

3

4

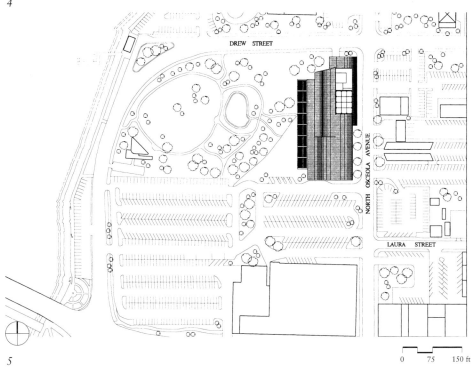

5

DREW STREET

NORTH OSCEOLA AVENUE

LAURA STREET

0   75   150 ft

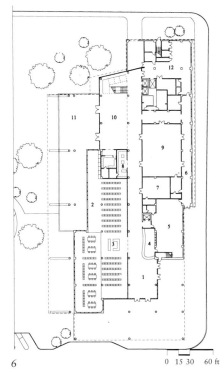

6

0 15 30   60 ft

Perkins Visitor Center
Wave Hill

Riverdale, The Bronx, New York
1998–2003

390   Wave Hill, a cultural institution offering
educational programs in the arts and the
sciences, is known both for innovative
gardens and for splendid views
overlooking the Hudson River and the
New Jersey Palisades. We will transform
an existing garage into a visitor center;
a 1930s addition to the garage will give
way to a new board-and-batten courtyard
building for the garden staff.

1. *Aerial view*
2. *Site plan*
3. *Plan*

1

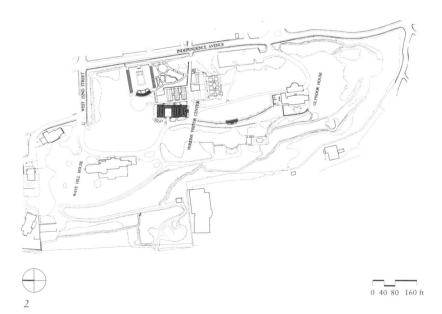

0 40 80 160 ft

2

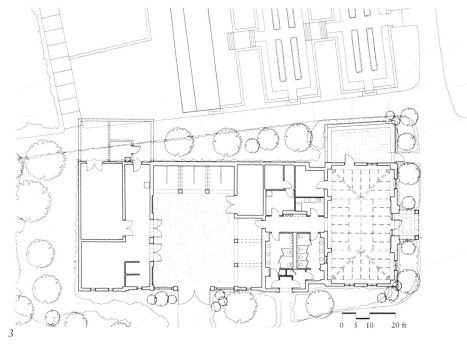

3

0   5   10   20 ft

1

Product Design

2001–2002

Inspired by the classic Greek-key pattern, our second collection for Sasaki includes dinnerware decorated at the rim, glassware with incised and sandblasted decorations, and flatware with a surprising twist of asymmetry.

Our EXchange collection for HBF Textiles brings the character of residential interior design to public contract furnishings. The collection is primarily figural, with texture and weave playing a supporting role.

1. *Sasaki Hydra stemware, Corinth dinnerware, and Greek Key flatware on HBF PLaza fabric*
2. *Sasaki Hydra barware, Thebes bowl, and Thera coaster on HBF GRamercy fabric*
3. *HBF KLondike, BUtterfield, ALgonquin, PLaza, and JUdson fabrics*
4. *HBF BUtterfield, GRamercy, ALgonquin, and KLondike fabrics*
5. *HBF JUdson, BUtterfield, PLaza, KLondike, and GRamercy fabrics*
6. *HBF GRamercy, PLaza, ALgonquin, and BUtterfield fabrics*

2

3

5

4

6

Classroom Academic Building and Communications Technology Complex Indiana University/Purdue University

Indianapolis, Indiana
1998–2003

394 Forming the northeast corner of a new academic quadrangle at the gateway to IUPUI's sprawling post–World War II campus, the 207,000-square-foot Classroom Academic Building and Communications Technology Complex houses the university's principal information-technology offices and programs, including the global operations center for Internet2, the Indiana Pervasive Computing Research Center, and other academic, laboratory, and administrative functions, as well as classrooms and offices for the Schools of Music, Library and Information Sciences, and Informatics. The two wings of the building intersect in a four-story atrium that serves as a naturally illuminated entrance connecting public streets to the quadrangle. This arrangement was initially adopted to permit the building to be realized in two phases, although in the end funding was found to build both wings at once.

Our design develops and refines the architectural language of the campus, established by ten Edward Larrabee Barnes buildings, including the library (1993). It combines different textures of limestone, large lightly tinted windows, and silver-gray metal detailing. On the fifth floor, a pergola shades a south-facing faculty roof terrace. A curving glass wall at the first and second floors brings natural light to student lounge and study areas adjacent to classrooms.

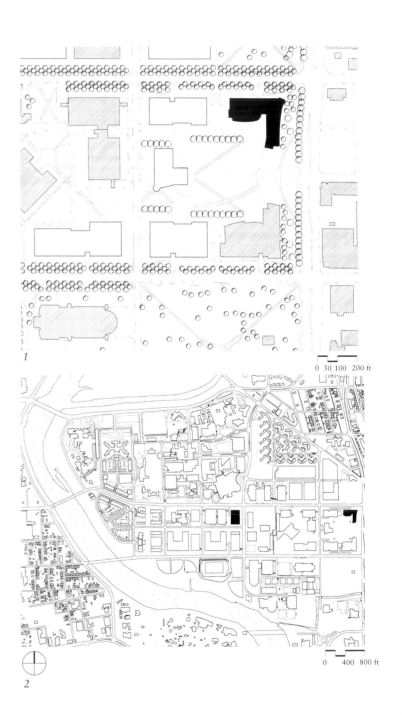

1

0 50 100 200 ft

2

0   400 800 ft

1. Site plan
2. Campus plan
3. Quadrangle
   entrance from
   southwest
4. Public street
   entrance from
   northeast
5. First-floor plan

395

3

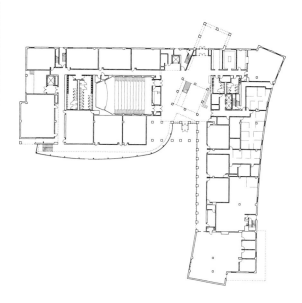

4

5

Dean's Loft

New Haven, Connecticut
1998–1999

1. *View from across Chapel Street*
2. *Main-level plan*
3. *Upper-level plan*
4. *Chapel Street facade*

396   I was appointed the dean of the Yale School of Architecture in 1998 and the next year completed this loft to serve as a residence and as a setting for informal entertaining and discussion. The third-story walk-up duplex enjoys a commanding view of the New Haven Green at the front and an equally compelling view toward the helical ramps of a parking garage at the back. The loft is furnished with the work of designers who inspired me in my student days at Yale, as well as pieces by Yale-trained masters such as George Nelson, Eero Saarinen, and Norman Foster.

1

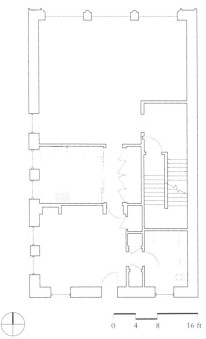

0   4   8   16 ft

2

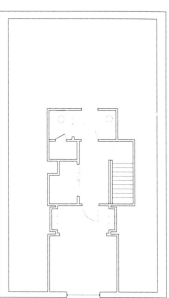

3

398

5

6

7. Living room
8. Entry hall

7, 8

Residence

Tidewater, Virginia
1999–

402 Occupying a wooded headland site with panoramic views of Hampton Roads and the James River, this shingled house contrasts a broadly gabled main mass and a less imposing service wing. The plan is configured so that most rooms offer views in two or more directions.

1. East elevation
2. Site plan
3. First-floor plan
4. View from
   northwest

1

2 ⊗

0 30 60   120 ft

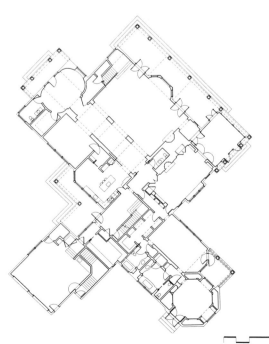

3

4

0   6   12   24 ft

Campus Community Center
Mission Bay Campus
University of California,
San Francisco

San Francisco, California
Competition, 1999

404   The competition for the Campus Community Center proposed a meeting and gathering place for all members of UCSF's new Mission Bay Campus and, in certain respects, for residents of this evolving south San Francisco neighborhood. The 242,000-square-foot building opens to the northeast onto a gently sloping greensward and to the northwest to an active outdoor recreation area for tennis and basketball. Its southwestern and southeastern facades open, respectively, to a surface parking lot proposed as the site of a future parking structure and to a neighboring laboratory building.

Our design is framelike, glassy and transparent, contrasting with the solid masonry facades with punched windows that will characterize the planned laboratory buildings. The center's inherently boxy mass is sculpted in response to the complex program, which is organized to provide both an energetic social focus for the building and adequate separation between functions that are at times antithetical. A covered arcade runs the full length of the northeastern and northwestern facades, offering access from the future parking garage to entrances to the fitness center, conference center, and student services. Wide south-facing terraces open off the center's second-floor dining areas and fifth floor student health facilities, while a north-facing terrace fronting on a large meeting room opens to views of the tennis and basketball courts.

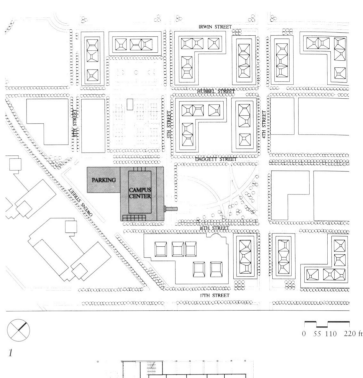

1

0 55 110   220 ft

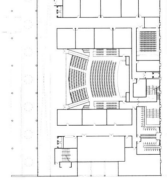

2

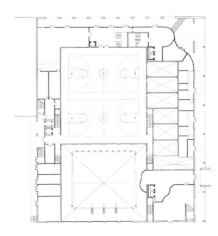

3

0 12.5 25   50 ft

4

5

Bryant Landing Senior Residence

Roslyn, New York
1999–

406 This full-service independent- and assisted-living facility, located on a prominent site overlooking Hempstead Harbor adjacent to Roslyn's commercial district, provides apartments and suites for three hundred residents, grand dining rooms and lounges, porches, and colonnaded walkways. A pedestrian promenade makes a visually coherent connection between the downtown and the waterfront, which has been lacking for generations. In order to relate to Roslyn village's late-eighteenth- and early-nineteenth-century character, the sprawling white-painted clapboard building is articulated as a series of wings that define garden courtyards.

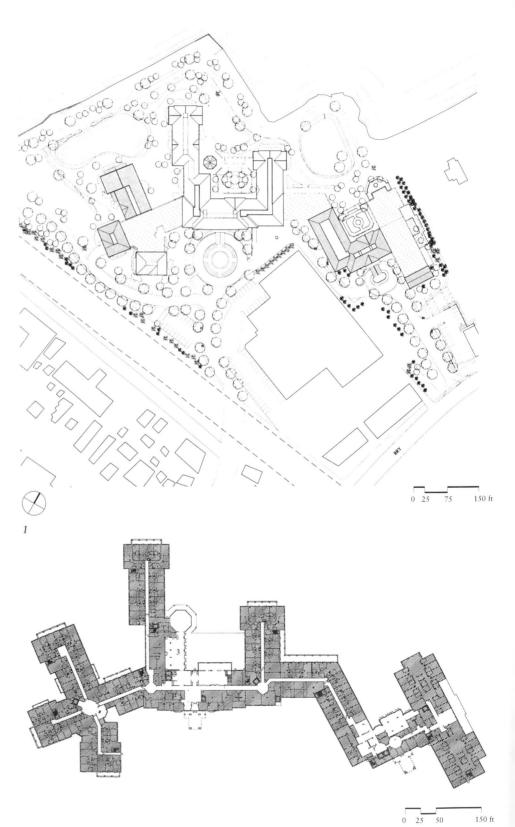

1

0 25 75   150 ft

0 25 50   150 ft

2

3

4

Zubiarte Retail and Leisure Center

Bilbao, Spain
1999–

408   A key element in the revitalization of the city's riverfront, Zubiarte (Basque for "near the bridge") forms part of Cesar Pelli's master plan for the area of land immediately to the west of Frank Gehry's Guggenheim. Zubiarte extends the Ensanche, the nineteenth-century street grid of Bilbao, with new north-south streets realized as glass-covered pedestrian arcades that, as they lead to the river, break up the big block into four distinct buildings. Although Zubiarte shares the rectilinear discipline of the Ensanche, it addresses the river with a sense of individualism: a sweeping arc of terraces and broad flights of stairs interact with a new waterfront boulevard and promenade. Visitors crossing the Puente de Deusto, one of the city's principal entry points, are welcomed into the building under a boldly cantilevered glass marquee.

1. *Site plan*
2. *Upper-level plan*
3. *Interior view*
4. *View from Puente de Deusto*
5. *View from north-west*

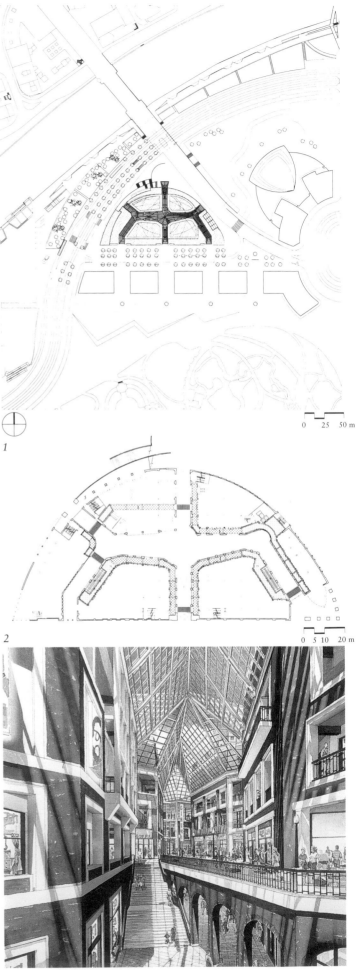

1

2

3

4

5

John L. Vogelstein '52
Dormitory
Taft School

Watertown, Connecticut
1999–2002

410   The Taft School was designed, first by
Bertram G. Goodhue and then by
James Gamble Rogers, as a superscale,
multiwinged, stylistically unified
red-brick and limestone Gothic Revival
structure, modeled after the colleges
at Oxford and Cambridge. During the
1960s, the school strayed from both the
language and the single-building planning
strategy of its founding architects; the
historic language was reembraced in the
1980s, and with our addition, so was
the idea of a single building. This new
wing provides dormitory rooms for forty-
eight students along with four faculty
apartments, four common rooms,
and three classrooms. The four-story,
red-brick, buff-cast-stone-trimmed,
graded-slate-roofed wing is connected to
Charles Phelps Taft Hall (James Gamble
Rogers, 1929), with which it frames a
south-facing courtyard. The north facade
of the new wing opens to the school's
playing fields and to distant rural views,

1. *Site plan*
2. *New quadrangle
with Charles
Phelps Hall
(left) and new
dormitory (right)*

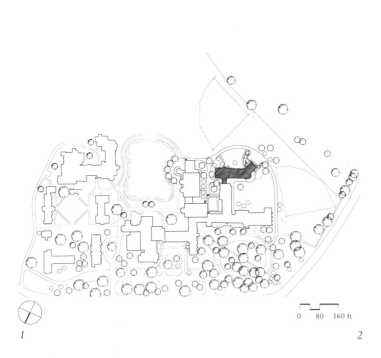

0   80   160 ft

1

2

3, 4

3. South facade
4. Arcade bridge link-
   ing new dormitory
   to Charles Phelps
   Taft Hall

while a short spur at the eastern end
parallels the adjacent street to open
the newly formed courtyard to morning
sunlight.

Each of the new residence hall's four
floors contains a neighborhood of
between ten and twelve single rooms
that can be combined to form two-room
suites. A single bathroom on each floor
permits coed use but is consistent with
Taft's intention that each neighborhood
be occupied by one sex only. On the first
three floors, a student lounge is located
within an octagonal tower; on the top
floor, the lounge is located at the
northeastern corner to command views
of the Connecticut hills. The top of the
tower is home to the building's one
desirable double room.

5. Interior of bridge
6. Main stair
7. First-floor plan
8. Ground-floor plan
9. Main entrance

5

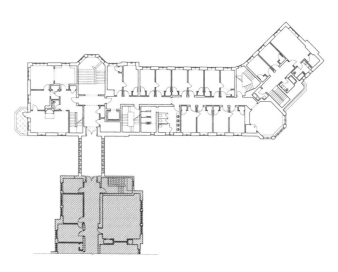

7

6

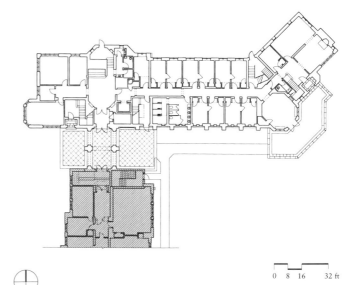

8

0 8 16   32 ft

10. *Faculty apartment*
11. *Typical student room*
12. *Fourth-floor lounge*

10

11

12

626 West Main
Louisville, Kentucky
1999–2002

418   This project for the Brown-Forman Corporation is located within Louisville's Main Street historic district. 626 West Main combines the restoration of a six-story late-nineteenth-century bourbon warehouse, known locally as the Bernheim Building, with the construction of a wing facing Seventh Street and a new two-story entry pavilion containing a double-height, skylighted, 2,300-square-foot courtyard that serves as the new building's lobby and as a place for special events. Materials for the expansion, intended to complement the deep red Minnesota sandstone, gauged brick, and terra cotta of the original, include red Cumbrian sandstone, smooth red brick, painted steel, and painted wood.

1

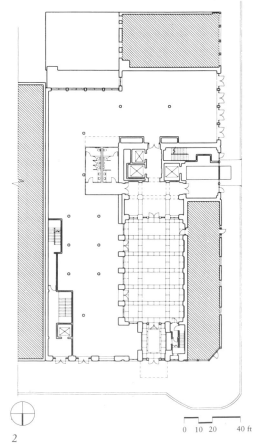

0 10 20   40 ft

2

1. View from
   northwest
2. Ground-floor
   plan
3. Model view
   from north

419

3

Residence in Bel Air

Los Angeles, California
1999–2003

420 Perched nine hundred feet above Los Angeles on a terraced site with panoramic views of the city, the Pacific Ocean, and the mountains to the west, this white-painted brick Regency house, inspired by the work of mid-twentieth-century architect Paul Williams and interior designer Billy Haines, evokes the casual glamour of the black-and-white movies of Hollywood's heyday. House and garden are designed as one: a carefully orchestrated sequence of spaces, which starts with the broad central gallery, runs the length of the house parallel to the southerly views, leading past the living room with its dramatic vista of sloping lawn to an elliptical garden and then to a hidden garden where, on a lower terrace twenty feet below the house, a pavilion overlooks a horizon swimming pool hovering above the city.

1. *North (entry) elevation*
2. *South (garden) elevation of house and pool pavilion*
3. *Site plan*
4. *First-floor plan*

1

2

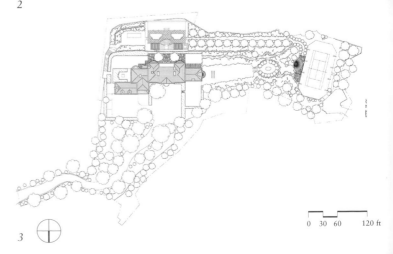

3

0 30 60   120 ft

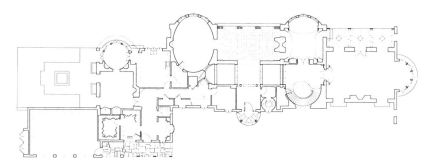

0 5 10   20 ft

4

A. James Clark Hall
Whitaker Biomedical
Engineering Institute
Johns Hopkins University

Baltimore, Maryland
1999–2001

422 This fifty-five-thousand-square-foot
building on the wooded western flank
of the university's Homewood Campus
opens to a broad greensward that will
form the heart of a future quadrangle.
Clark Hall draws on the architectural
heritage of the campus, specifically that
of the engineering quadrangle, where
eight buildings erected over a period
of more than half a century share a
common stone-trimmed red-brick
Georgian vocabulary. The building is
articulated as two slate-roofed pavilions,
de-emphasizing its length while permitting
a simple double-loaded plan. Naturally
lighted at both ends, a central corridor is
punctuated at its midpoint by a three-
story open stair rising from a stone-paved
ground-floor lobby. Flanked by meeting
rooms, lounges, and kitchenettes, the
corridor accommodates requirements for
modular, reconfigurable laboratories
while functioning as an effective social
condenser, bringing together members
of various research groups who had
previously worked in dispersed facilities.

1. *Site plan*
2. *East facade*
3. *Ground-floor plan*
4. *Stair hall*
5. *Laboratory*

2

1

0   100   200 ft

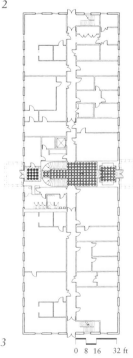

3

0 8 16   32 ft

4

5

Residence at West Tisbury

Martha's Vineyard, Massachusetts
1999–2003

424 This casually composed house, which commands views north across Vineyard Sound, groups various elements around a wind-sheltered south-facing courtyard overlooking a meadow, orchard, and pond restored after fifty years of neglect. In keeping with the effort to restore the historic character of this land, we studied vernacular buildings on the Vineyard and on Cape Cod to inform both the composition and the detailing of the new house and its outbuildings. Guest and staff quarters and the garage, together with a pool pavilion, create a small compound between the main house and the beach.

1. *South (entry) elevation*
2. *Site plan*
3. *First-floor plan*

1

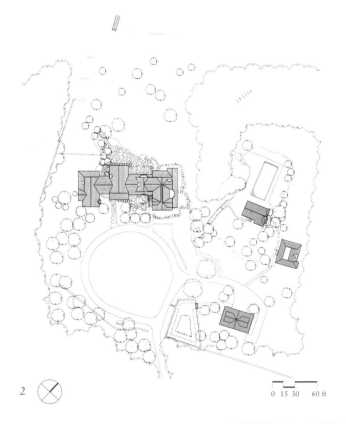

2

0 15 30   60 ft

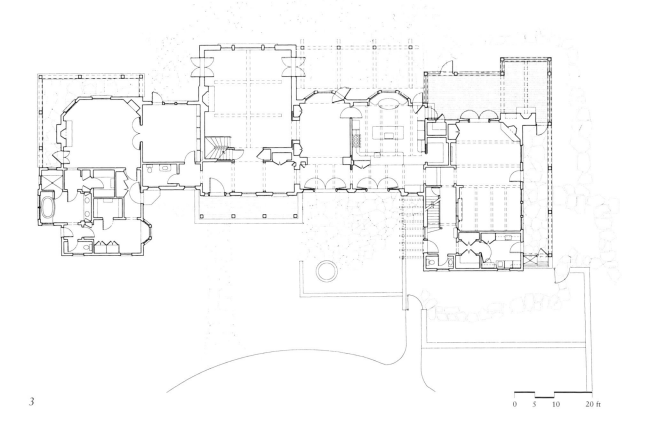

3

0   5   10   20 ft

Arnhem City Center

Arnhem, The Netherlands
1999–

426   This 9,600-square-meter mixed-use project on the Brouwerstraat is the centerpiece of an effort to reclaim a formerly industrial part of the city by creating a market square surrounded by new buildings, combining ground-floor retail and residential space above, carefully woven into and around historic buildings in an idiom that complements but does not mimic them. A glass-covered arcade offers shelter during long, rainy Dutch winters and provides an important connection from the established shopping destination Land van de Markt to the new market square.

1. *Retail passage*
2. *Site plan*
3. *Entry to retail passage*
4. *Plaza*

1

2

0 5 10   20m

3

4

Bearings

Seal Harbor, Maine
1999–2002

428   Perched on a granite bluff overlooking Bear Island, a guest house and squash house, the first components of a residential compound on a magnificent site on Mount Desert Island in Maine, are located along the western side of the property to create a buffer from neighbors and to reserve a large open site at the highest part of the property for a future main house. The buildings, at slight angles to one another, are organized around a pool terrace to the south and a hedge-enclosed tennis court to the north. A curved porch at the eastern end of the squash house looks obliquely across the pool toward the mouth of Northeast Harbor.

1. Site plan
2. Guest house and
  squash house
  looking northwest

0 16 32   64 ft

1

2

3. *Guest house looking south*
4. *Squash house porch*
5. *Pool and guest house looking west*

3

4

5

6. *Squash court*
   viewing gallery
7. *Second-floor plan*
8. *First-floor plan*
9. *Squash court*

6

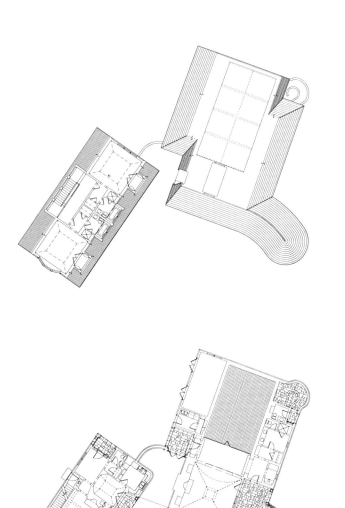

7

8

0 4 8   16 ft

10

11

12

Jesse H. Jones Graduate School of Business Management Rice University

Houston, Texas
1999–2002

438   The 160,000-square-foot new home for Rice University's business school is located on a prominent site near the western end of campus. It faces the James A. Baker III Institute of Public Policy (Hammond, Beeby & Babka Architects, 1997) to the south and Alice Pratt Brown Hall (Ricardo Bofill Taller de Arquitectura, 1991) to the west. The scope of our work included a master plan for a quadrangle to be bounded by these buildings and as yet undeveloped sites as well as the design of the Jones School building and a two-level, 486-car parking garage below.

The symmetrical front facade of the Jones School mirrors the mass, scale, and general proportions of the Baker Institute but expresses the program within with a second-floor, double-height arcade that screens the reading room of the library. The balance of the building's considerable mass is placed in a slipped-bar arrangement of east-west classroom and office wings punctuated where they overlap by an open-air sallyport that facilitates pedestrian movement through the building.

The Jones School offers both graduate and executive education programs. On the ground floor, common amenities such as a 208-seat dining room and student, faculty, and executive lounges surround a courtyard. Also on the ground floor and adjacent to the main entrance are the school's placement office and a five-hundred-seat auditorium. On the second and third floors, the library, classrooms, and faculty offices are configured to foster collegial interaction. In addition to sixty-seat tiered case-study rooms, the new building features an instructional trading room and "dinner theaters," tiered classrooms with six-person tables that permit students to listen to a single presenter and to work in small groups.

Like other Rice buildings, the Jones School exterior is clad in St. Joe's brick

1

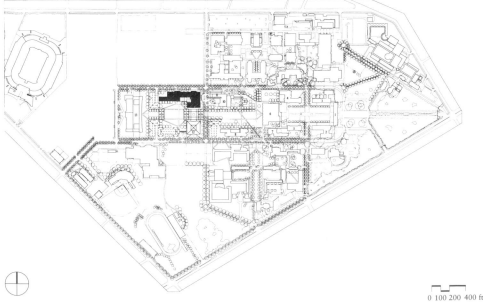

2

0 100 200 400 ft

1. View north across Jamail Plaza
2. Campus plan
3. Facade detail
4. Jamail Plaza entry

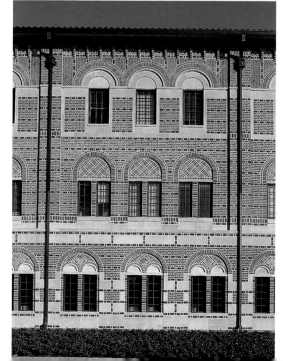

3, 4

5. *View from east*
6. *Facade detail*
7. *North facade*

5

6

with wide, flat struck joints, limestone and matching cast-stone trim, a Missouri granite base, and red barrel-tile roofs. The details and massing explicitly recall Lovett Hall (Cram, Goodhue & Ferguson, 1912), among other earlier buildings. Jones Hall continues the university's long tradition of architectural iconography with Kent Bloomer's plaques and cameos depicting famous and infamous business practitioners and theoreticians through the ages.

7

8. *Lobby at second floor*
9. *First-floor plan*
10. *Stair*

8

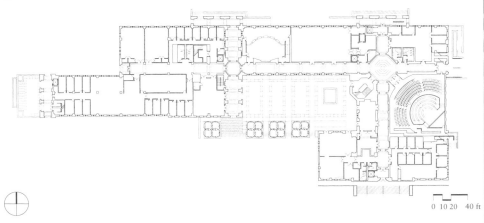

9

0 10 20 40 ft

10

11. Library
12. Study corridor
13. Library

11

12

13

14. *Shell Oil Foundation*
    Auditorium
15. *Office*
16. *Breakout rooms*

    Overleaf
17. *View across Woodson*
    Courtyard

14, 15

16

The Westminster

180 West 20th Street
New York, New York
1999–2002

450 This 15-story, 270,000-square-foot, 254-unit apartment building employs shapes, patterns, and detailing that relate to neighboring Art Deco buildings. Its massing is broken down into "towers" and recesses to further integrate into the context. The ground floor is clad in limestone, while the upper floors are sheathed in gold-colored brick with brown and black accents. The residential entrance is detailed in satin-finished stainless steel, and the public spaces have Cipollino marble floors, pearwood paneling, and stucco veneziano walls. The roof garden was inspired by Deco-era ocean liners.

1

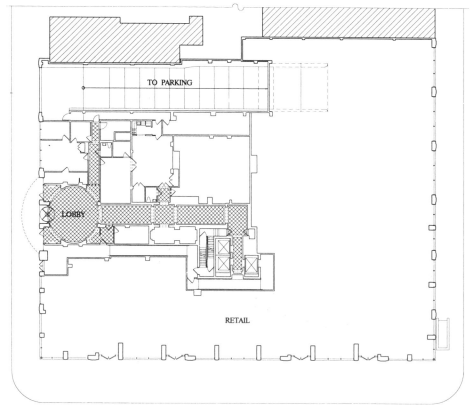

2

0   15   30 ft

THE WESTMINSTER

4

4. Lobby
5. Elevator lobby
6. Elevator cab
7. Concierge desk
8. Plan for floors
   four and five
9. Typical corridor

5, 6

7

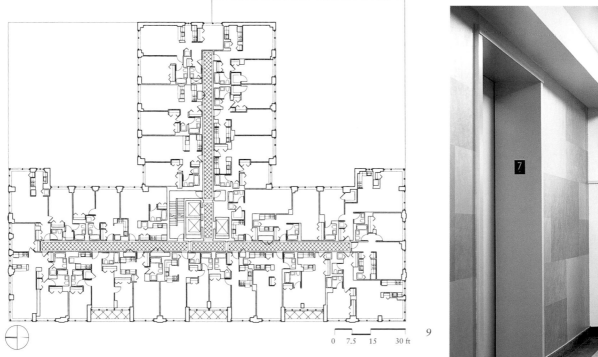

8

0 7.5 15 30 ft

9

10. *Roof garden
    looking east*
11. *Roof garden
    looking south*

10

11

479 Thornall Avenue

Edison Township, New Jersey
1999–

456 This eleven-story, three-hundred-thousand-square-foot office building will join two existing structures to define a greensward and paved plaza facing the northeast rail corridor one block from the MetroPark train station. The undulating glass facade, which appears to push through the cubic volume of the building, promises a distinct identity for the complex as a whole.

1

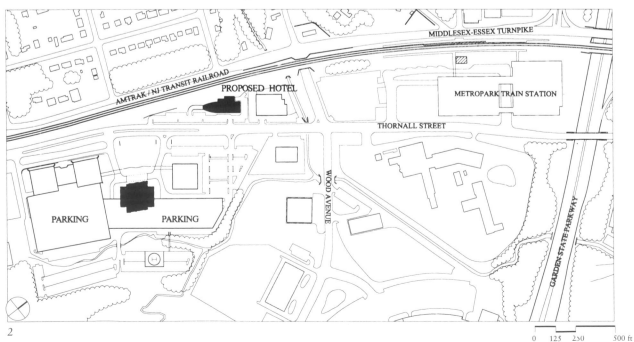

2

0   125   250   500 ft

1. *Model view look-*
   ing southeast
2. *Site plan*
3. *Ground-floor plan*
4. *Plan of floors*
   three through ten

457

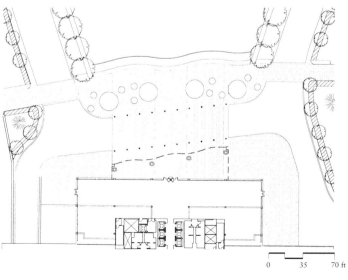

0   35   70 ft

3

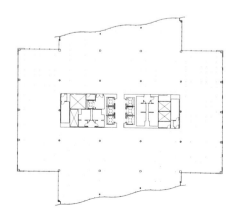

4

Residence in Edgartown

Martha's Vineyard, Massachusetts
1999–2003

1. Detail at south
   facade
2. First-floor plan
3. North (entry)
   facade
4. South (garden)
   facade

458   The goal of this three-phase renovation project was to provide traditional scale and hierarchy to a sprawling, architecturally undistinguished house deemed too new to tear down. An existing one-story entry was replaced with a two-story gambrel-roofed addition that contains a spacious hall, staircase, and library on the first floor and a master suite upstairs. The loftlike living, dining, and kitchen wing was reworked to provide discrete rooms and a new south-facing dining-room pavilion. Windows were replaced with large, simple double-hung units; detailed trim throughout transforms the shingled house into a Shingle-style house. A new pool house and spa building were designed in the style of the cottages found on the picturesque streets of Edgartown.

1

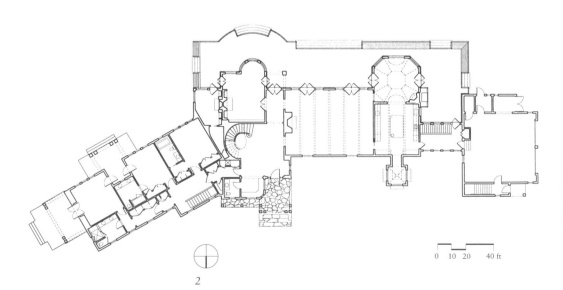

0   10   20   40 ft

2

3

4

Residence

*Salt Spring Island,
British Columbia, Canada
1999–*

460 Part of the charm of Salt Spring Island is
its isolation: it is accessible only by ferry
or seaplane. The southern tip of Scott
Point, a narrow peninsula, provides a
secluded spot for this house; the site
offers panoramic views of both Ganges
and Long Harbours and the neighboring
islands, all animated by the comings and
goings of ferries and planes. Along with
the U-shaped main house, which wraps
around an entrance courtyard sheltered
from the strong, often cold, prevailing
southerly winds, included in the design
are a boathouse to the east on Long
Harbour, a teahouse to the west adjacent
to the entrance drive overlooking Ganges
Harbour, and a spa pavilion at the south
end of the point.

*1. South elevation
2. Site plan
3. First-floor plan*

1

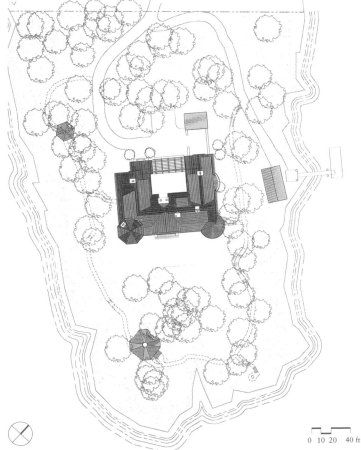

2

0 10 20   40 ft

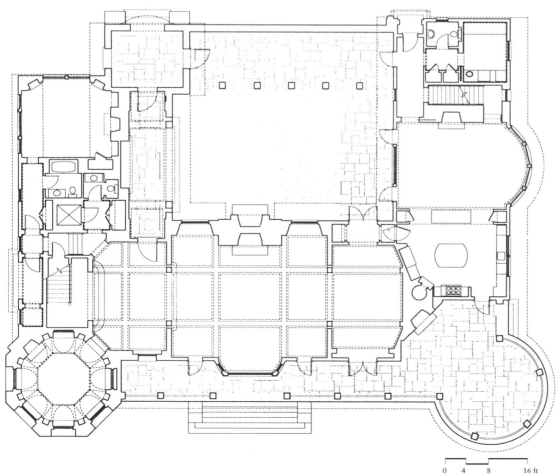

0   4   8   16 ft

K. C. Irving Environmental Science Centre and Harriet Irving Botanical Gardens Acadia University

Wolfville, Nova Scotia, Canada
1998–2002

1. Site plan
2. Main entry
3. Main entry from
   University Avenue

Overleaf
4. View from
   graduation lawn

462 Sited at the northern edge of a new seven-acre botanical garden is our first project at Acadia University, the sixty-five-thousand-square-foot K. C. Irving Environmental Science Centre, which combines facilities for scientific research and instruction with meeting and gathering spaces that will bring all members of the university community into contact with the natural sciences. With its red brick, granite water table, limestone trim, and slate roof, the Environmental Science Centre looks to the restrained Georgian classicism of the university's older buildings. The building's state-of-the-art greenhouse draws its form from the rich history of glass houses and conservatories. To the south, the greenhouse opens to a walled garden, graduation lawn, and research garden that are part of the new Harriet Irving Botanical Gardens, dedicated to the study of the native flora of the Acadia region. The three-story building terminates visual and pedestrian axes that focus on the campus's historic University Hall and Student Centre.

Immediately adjacent to the Irving Centre's lobby, a garden room for major receptions and other ceremonial gatherings opens to the walled garden. The building's lower level contains a 130-seat high-tech auditorium with adjacent breakout rooms and classrooms, while the upper level contains the Acadia Room, a 2,400-square-foot reception suite that serves as a meeting area for the board of trustees and offers views across the campus to the Bay of Fundy.

Laboratory and research facilities are distributed between the greenhouse on the main floor and lower-level laboratories. A 4,500-square-foot herbarium, designed to the highest archival standards, serves a growing collection of four hundred thousand preserved botanical specimens dating back to the eighteenth century.

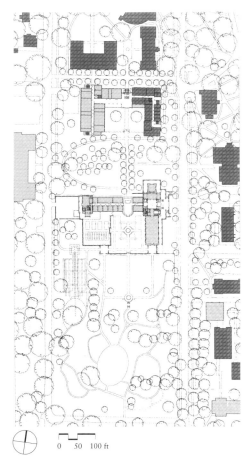

0 50 100 ft

1

2

3

5. Walled garden
6. Walled garden look-
   ing to greenhouse
7. Pavilion entrance
   to walled garden

5, 6

7

8. Lobby oculus at
   second floor
9. Second-floor plan
10. Ground-floor plan
11. Lower-floor plan
12. Lobby

8

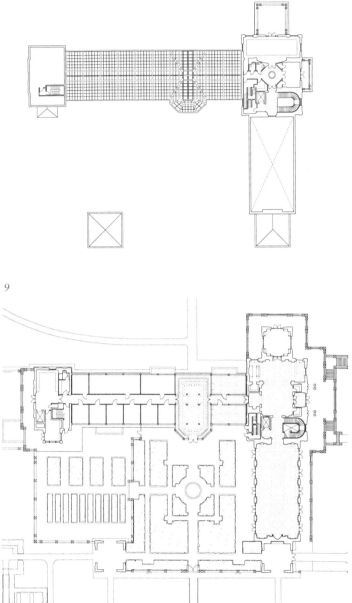

9

10

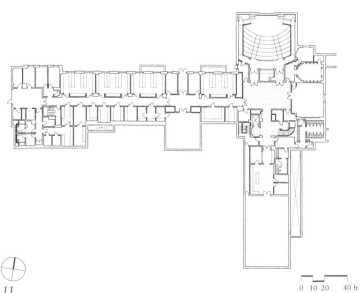

11

0 10 20   40 ft

13, 14

13. *Main stair looking*
   to garden room
14. *Main stair*
15. *Garden room*

16

17, 18

16. *Auditorium*
17. *Laboratory*
18. *Second-floor lobby alcove overlooking garden room*
19. *Acadia Room*
20. *Seminar room*
21. *Library and video-conference room*

19

20, 21

22. *Greenhouse looking*
to walled garden
23. *North facade*

22

23

Campus Plan
Acadia University

Wolfville, Nova Scotia, Canada
1999–2000

1. Campus plan
2. Existing University Quadrangle
3. Proposed University Quadrangle
4. Existing Horton Drive
5. Proposed Horton Walk
6. Existing west gateway
7. Proposed west gateway
8. Existing south campus
9. Proposed south campus

476 With the design of the Irving Centre well under way in 1999, we were asked to continue our work for Acadia University with a master plan for the campus. Founded in 1839, Acadia, consistently rated Canada's best small liberal-arts university, had by the 1930s developed an attractive and well-planned campus with the support of local donors and the Carnegie and Rockefeller Foundations. After World War II, the university entered a period characterized by a lack of planning and generally lowered architectural standards.

Our plan for the campus strengthens its pedestrian character by intensifying development at the core. It resists campus sprawl by siting new buildings among existing ones to form academic quadrangles and residential colleges; several postwar buildings that are both functionally and aesthetically deficient will be demolished. An ambitious campaign of land acquisition will strengthen the campus edges and provide for future needs, while an existing tract of forest will be preserved as a university-owned greenbelt that defines and protects the campus's southern and western flanks.

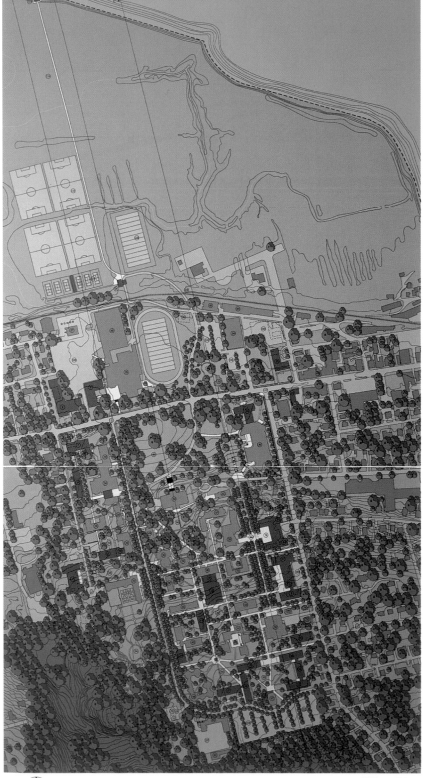

1

0 100 200   400 ft

2

3

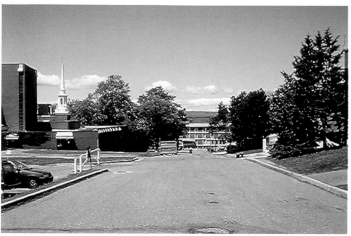

4

5

6

7

8

9

Residence Advantage Plan Acadia University

Wolfville, Nova Scotia, Canada
1999–

478 In January 2001, we were asked to begin implementing our campus plan by guiding the Acadia Residence Advantage Plan, a seven-year campaign to increase the number of students living on campus by converting the university to a residential-college system through the renovation of nearly all residence halls on campus and the building of six new ones and commons for each of the five newly formed colleges. The first phase of the plan, completed in August 2001, consisted of the renovation of two strikingly different residence halls. Whitman House, a much-loved thirty-two-thousand-square-foot 1914 Arts and Crafts–style structure, was treated as a historic-preservation project; nevertheless, extensive changes included the addition of student rooms, two new entrances, and the reconfiguration of bathrooms and student lounges. The wholesale renovation and reconfiguration of Eaton House, on the other hand, transformed an unpopular 1970s building into a popular residence by dividing the forty-nine-thousand-square-foot, two-hundred-bed dormitory into two separate structures, Eaton House and Christofor Hall. Two more residence halls, Dennis House and Chipman House, were renovated for the fall 2002 term. Our work continues with one new residence hall and the first commons building.

1. Aerial view

2

2. *Eaton House*
   before renovation
3. *Christofor Hall*
   and Eaton House
   after renovation
4. *Christofor Hall*
   main lounge

3

5

5. Chipman House
   south facade after
   renovation
6. Chipman House
   before renovation
7. Chipman House
   main corridor
   after renovation
8. Chipman House
   main corridor
   before renovation

6

483

7

8

9

9. *Dennis House south facade after renovation*
10. *Dennis House before renovation*
11. *Aerial view of Dennis House before renovation*
12. *Aerial view of Dennis House after renovation*

10

11

13

13. *Dennis House
    main lounge after
    renovation*
14. *Dennis House
    main lounge
    before renovation*
15. *Dennis House
    main lounge
    before renovation*
16. *Dennis House
    floor lounge after
    renovation*

14

15

Residence Hall
Brooklyn Law School

Brooklyn, New York
2000–2003

488   This new residence hall, located on the corner of Boerum and State Streets, will meet the needs of law students, many returning to school after other careers, with 385 apartment-like units. Shared social spaces include a multipurpose student lounge on the ground floor and conference facilities at the top of the building. Classical detailing and limestone trim will visually connect the new building to the academic tower we designed for the school in 1994, but rose-colored brick will identify the building as a residence.

1

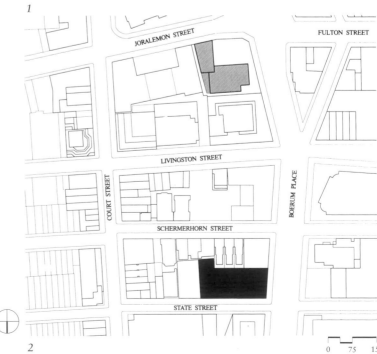

2

0   75   150 ft

3

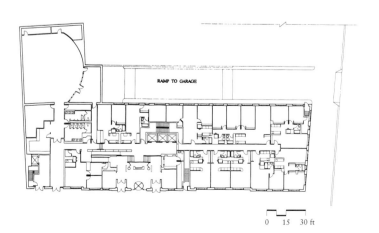

4

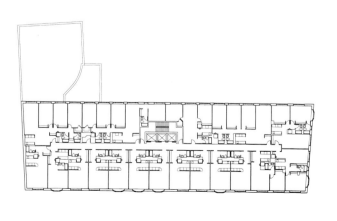

0   15   30 ft

5

Nathaniel R. Jones
Federal Building and
United States Courthouse

Youngstown, Ohio
2000–2002

490 Historic Youngstown consists of three distinct but interdependent districts: to the south, the remains of steelworks from the nineteenth century sprawl along the Mahoning River; to the north, up Wick Avenue on the heights, are various cultural institutions, including the Butler Art Museum (McKim, Mead & White, 1910), Youngstown State University, and many of the city's places of assembly; and in the valley in between lies the business and civic core, with many commercial offices located in miniskyscrapers of the 1920s and government buildings grouped near Federal Square. The bold curve of the new Jones Federal Building and U.S. Courthouse dramatically fills the yawning gap along Wick Avenue between the commercial core and the cultural heights.

A ceremonial public stair visible behind the colonnaded window wall leads to the building's single courtroom, which is located on the third floor to acknowledge its importance in the composition. Light wells between the curving and rectilinear geometries bring natural light into the courtroom without compromising stringent federal security requirements. Buff-colored brick, limestone trim, metal columns and windows, and a projecting metal standing-seam roof carried on metal brackets reflect the classical stone buildings and industrial architecture characteristic of Youngstown's heritage.

1. *View to First Presbyterian Church from plaza, with Andrew Leicester's* Phantom Furnace Columns
2. *First-floor plan*
3. *Entry from west*
4. *View from northwest*

1

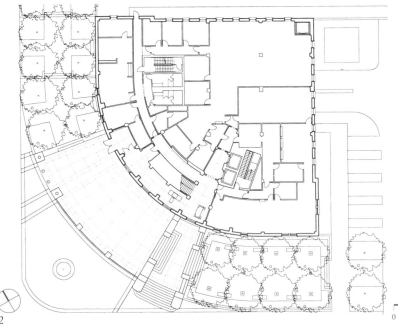

2

0   25   50 ft

3, 4

5. *Southwest facade*
6. *View from north*
7. *Stair from East Commerce Street*

6

7

8. Courtroom
9. Third-floor (court-
   room level) plan
10. Main stair

8

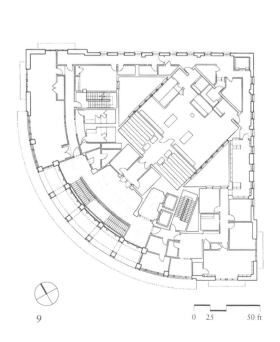

9

0   25   50 ft

Pennsylvania Plaza

Philadelphia, Pennsylvania
2000–

496 In 1987, the Liberty Place towers built by Pennsylvania-based Liberty Property Trust transformed Philadelphia's skyline by breaking the unofficial height barrier set by the statue of William Penn atop City Hall. In 2000, we were retained by Liberty to develop designs for a central two-acre site above Philadelphia's main commuter rail lines. Our first design was a 1.5-million-square-foot, 869-foot-tall, glass-clad hexagonal tower with three subtle setbacks. The proposed tower was to rise from a 25,000-square-foot ground-level winter garden.

A second design for the site was to launch a new era for the city's skyline with a 62-story, 1.7-million-square-foot office tower; at 1,030 feet, it would have been the tallest building in the United States outside of New York or Chicago. The tower's geometry derived from a square footprint at the base and a slightly smaller square roof plan rotated forty-five degrees from the base. The floorplates were chamfered squares that ranged in size from 20,600 to 28,800 square feet. The building's eight triangular facades of silver-gray glass canted alternately inward or outward, giving the building a constantly changing profile. Atriums thrust above the building, marking the skyline with a pair of light-filled glass rooms with clean, crystalline forms that stood out from the heavily articulated tops of Philadelphia's other recent skyscrapers.

Cost and tenant requirements led to a third iteration of the Pennsylvania Plaza development. Two new office buildings frame a south-facing plaza. The 1.4-million-square-foot central tower, One Pennsylvania Plaza, rises 804 feet and is set back from the boulevard behind the plaza and a 110-foot-high winter garden that serves both as a forecourt to the tower and as a light-flooded entrance to commuter trains. The tower is clad in golden Kasota stone and matching cast-stone panels on the upper floors, recalling the stone facades of the beloved Philadelphia Museum of Art (Horace

First Scheme
1. *View from Schuylkill River looking southwest*
2. *Site plan*
3. *View from steps of Philadelphia Museum of Art*

1

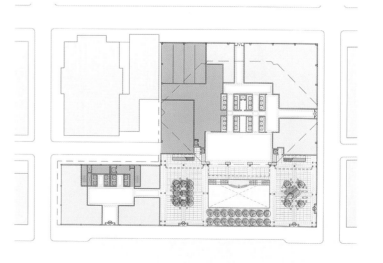

0   25   50 ft

2

Second Scheme
4. Cutaway axono-
   metrics
5. View from
   Schuylkill River
   looking southwest
6. Aerial view looking
   to Philadelphia
   Museum of Art

498

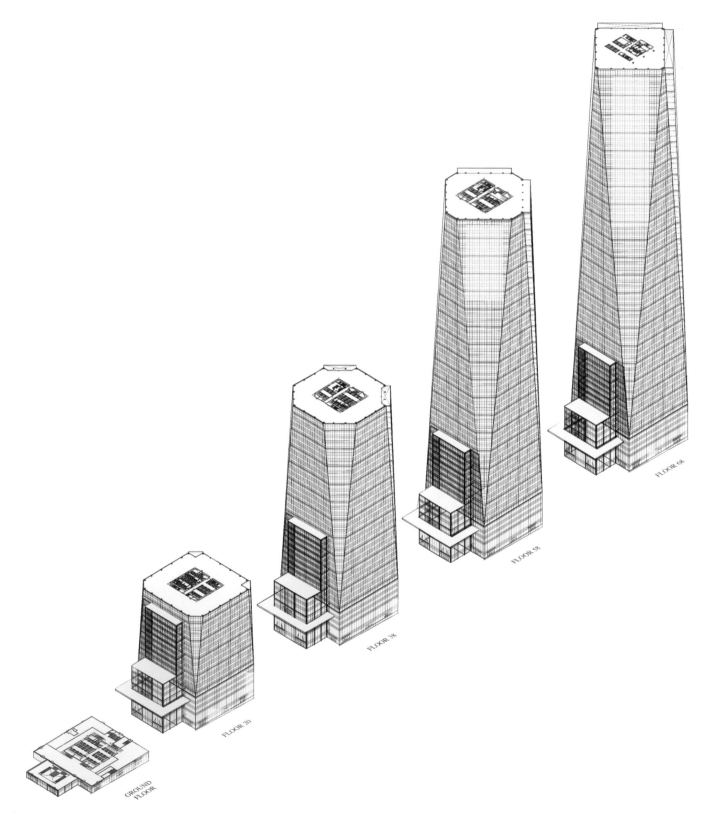

GROUND
FLOOR

FLOOR 20

FLOOR 38

FLOOR 58

FLOOR 68

4

.5

6

500

7

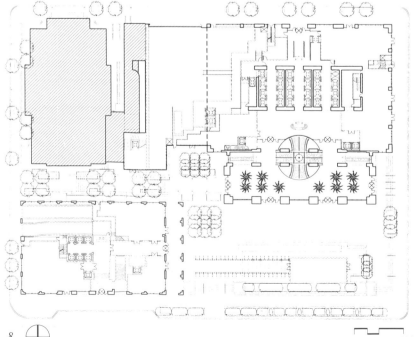

8

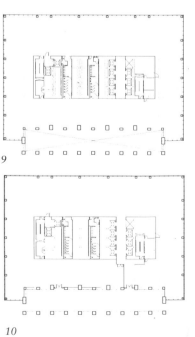

9

10

0   25   50 ft

502 Trumbauer, C. Clark Zantziger, and Charles L. Borie Jr., 1928). Stacked three-story "sky atrium" spaces overlook the plaza and provide greenery-filled common spaces. The 17-story, 280,000-square-foot Two Pennsylvania Plaza faces JFK Boulevard at the western edge of the plaza and, in its materials and scale, complements the historic train station to the east.

12

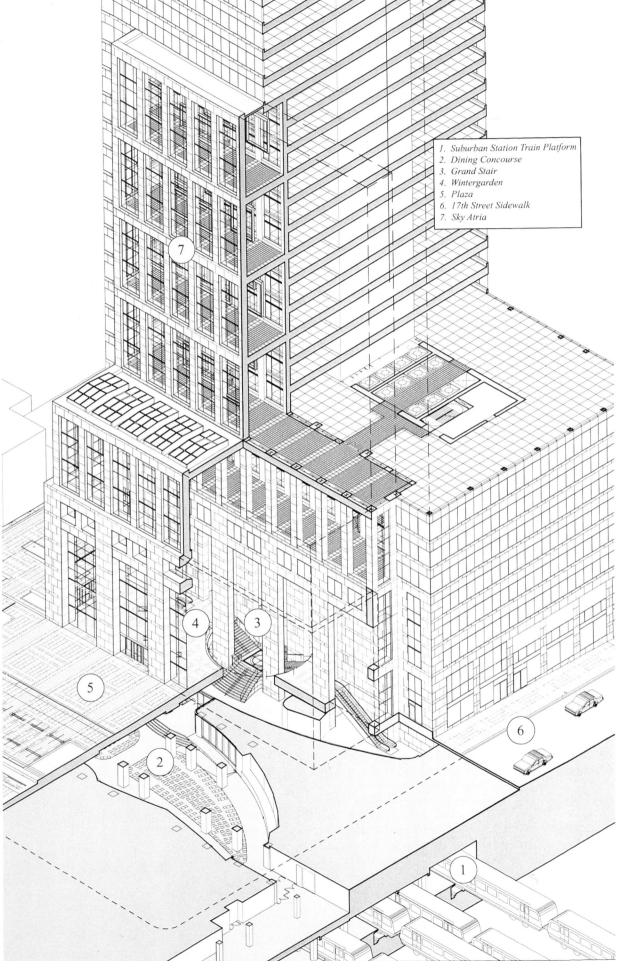

1. Suburban Station Train Platform
2. Dining Concourse
3. Grand Stair
4. Wintergarden
5. Plaza
6. 17th Street Sidewalk
7. Sky Atria

503

13

14. *Model view*
15. *Skyline view
    from Ben Franklin
    Bridge*

504

14

15

Residence and Office Building at Quartier am Tacheles

Berlin, Germany
2000–

1. Ground-floor plan
2. Site plan
3. Apartment building from northwest
4. Apartment building from southeast

506   For a new urban neighborhood master-planned by Duany Plater-Zyberk & Company on an important block at the end of the Friedrichstrasse in central Berlin, north of the River Spree, we were asked to propose two designs modeled on iconic New York buildings. A luxury apartment house in the spirit of the Beresford Apartments on Central Park West occupies its own block with a garden court at the center. An office building recalling the Flatiron Building is set on a triangular block between a shopping square and the Oranien-burgerstrasse. Plans are now proceeding for development of the apartment building.

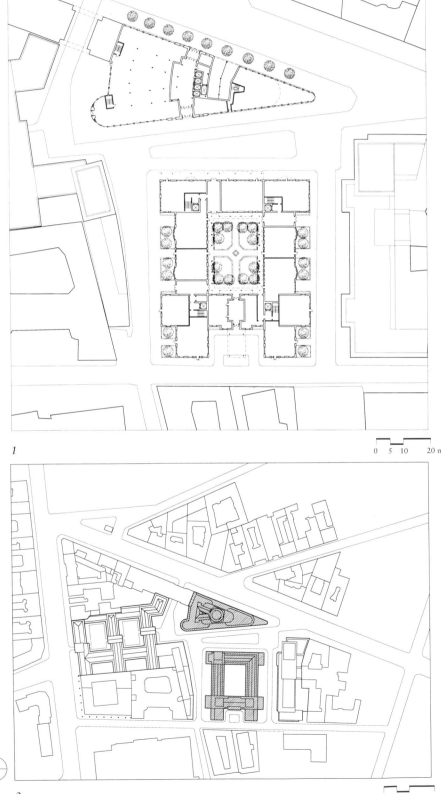

1

0 5 10   20 m

2

0 12.5 25   50 m

3

4

508   *5. Office building
       from southeast
       6. Office building
       and apartment
       bulding from
       northeast*

5

6

Master Plan
Bryn Mawr School

Baltimore, Maryland
2001–2002

1. *Existing campus plan*
2. *Proposed campus plan*
3. *Existing aerial view from south-west*
4. *Proposed aerial view from south-west*

510   Drawing inspiration from the original but barely realized master plan for the Bryn Mawr School, produced by Palmer & Lamdin in 1930, when the institution moved to the Orchards country estate from its original location in downtown Baltimore, the new plan reorganizes the school's four divisions. The Lower, Middle, and Upper Schools share the colonnaded quadrangle, as originally envisioned, while the Little School (the preschool) is set apart with historic Gordon House. The plan accommodates enlarged dining facilities as well as classrooms, laboratories, performance spaces, athletic facilities, and playing fields; it also reorganizes vehicular circulation, drop-offs, and parking. Just as important, it calls for the return to Palmer & Lamdin's regionally based classical vernacular as the basis for new buildings.

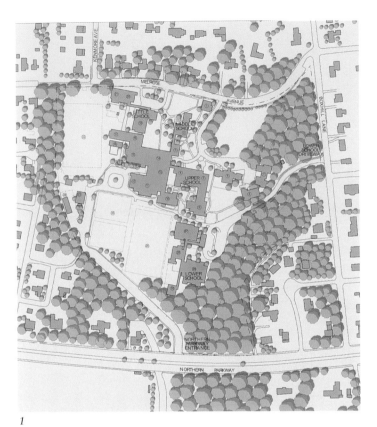

1

2   0 45 90 180 ft

3

4

512   *5. Proposed south*
       building (Upper
       School) from
       southeast
    6. Bryn Mawr Quad-
       rangle and pro-
       posed north build-
       ing (Middle School)

5

6

New Northrup Hall
Trinity University

San Antonio, Texas
2000–2003

1. First-floor plan
2. Site plan
3. View from northwest
4. Entry

514 Trinity University's "skyline campus" was laid out in 1952 by the noted architect O'Neil Ford, who designed many of its early buildings in a consistent modernist language of brick, metal, and glass. Later, as the university prospered and Ford's style evolved, he designed in a more regionalist manner, exemplified by Murchison Tower and Parker Chapel. Northrup Hall, built in 1952, was one of the first buildings on campus and was much added onto over the years; by 2000, it was something of a liability, interrupting vistas and paths. Trinity decided to replace it with a new building intended as a front door to the university that would frame Ford's tower and chapel, which had become the primary architectural focal points of the campus.

New Northrup will house a variety of student services, classrooms, two academic departments, and executive administration offices. Our design, selected in a four-firm competition, builds on and expands the architectural language of Ford's original vocabulary of sun-shading devices, covered walkways, and shade-intensive landscape that earned the campus its reputation as a showpiece of regionally responsive modernism.

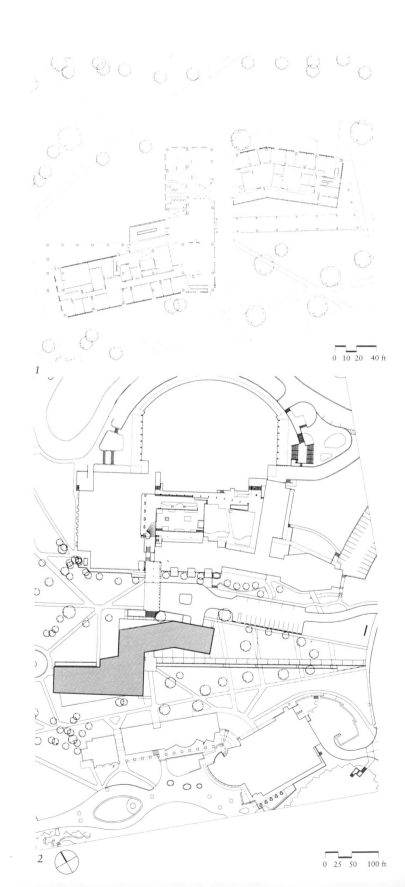

1

0 10 20 40 ft

2

0 25 50 100 ft

3

4

Residence

East Hampton, New York
2000–

516   This house replaces the owners' long-time residence with the French country–style house they had always wanted. Entry is through a garden courtyard on the north. On the south, two pavilions facing each other across an expansive garden and lawn frame the principal facade.

2

1

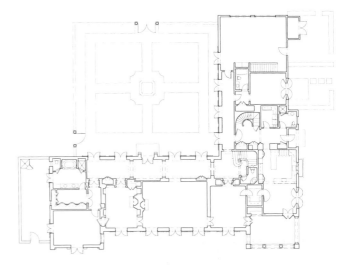

0   12.5   25   50 ft

0   5   10   20 ft

3

Hickey Freeman Shop

*666 Fifth Avenue,
New York, New York
2000–2001*

1. Entrance door
   pull
2. Entrance
   looking to
   Fifth Avenue
3. Plan
4. Display wall

518   Hickey Freeman is a venerable American men's clothing company that has sold its wares in men's specialty shops and department stores for a hundred years. This shop, the first built to showcase the company's line, reflects the heritage of the brand and the classic American style it represents. Our challenge was to transform a four-thousand-square-foot space that had previously been the lobby of a 1957 modernist building on a prime stretch of Fifth Avenue. Oversized Doric column surrounds mask the existing structural columns that support the building above. Abstracted coffering and beams provide a framework to organize and conceal the sophisticated lighting and mechanical equipment required for contemporary retailing. Beige walls and trim, French limestone floors, and limed oak cabinetry provide a warm yet neutral backdrop for display.

1

2

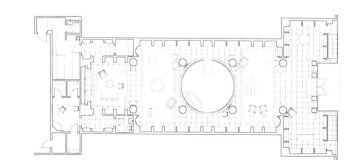

3

0 5 10   20 ft

5. *Ceiling detail*
6. *Custom clothing presentation area*
7. *Interior view looking west*

Overleaf
8. *Interior view looking north-west*

5

6

7

Main Library

Columbus, Georgia
2001–

1. *First-floor plan*
2. *Site plan*
3. *Entry facade*
4. *Section through rotunda and grand stair*

524 The key element in the redevelopment of a centrally located, forty-two-acre brownfield site formerly occupied by a shopping mall, this red-brick-and-limestone-clad three-story library rises to a lantern that will become a beacon for the city, visible from Interstate 185 and from surrounding neighborhoods. The new building will face busy Macon Road. A sweeping curve accommodating the principal reading rooms will overlook the park, as will a double-height, fifty-by-one-hundred-foot grand reading room with an outdoor balcony on the second floor.

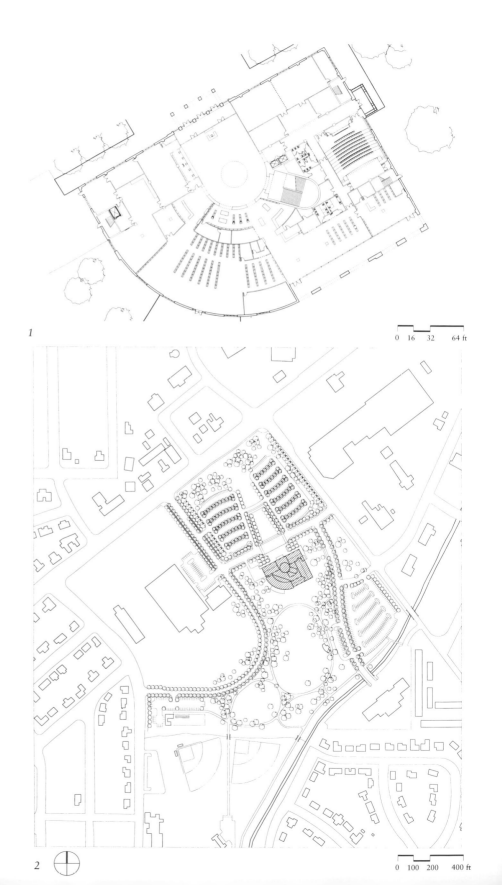

1

0   16   32   64 ft

2   ⊕

0   100   200   400 ft

3

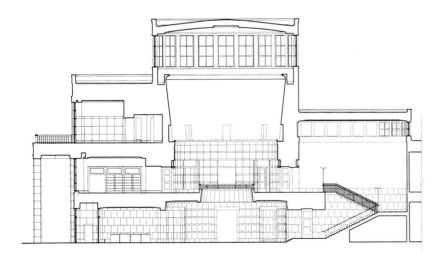

4

Education and Visitors Center
Mark Twain House

Hartford, Connecticut
2000–2003

526   The Mark Twain House (1874) is a masterpiece of the Queen Anne style designed by E. T. Potter for the author Samuel Clemens on a site in Nook Farm, a semirural enclave then on the fashionable outskirts of Hartford. By the end of the twentieth century, the site had been swamped by the city; most visitors currently approach the house from a drop-off area and parking lot located twenty-five feet below in what was in Clemens's lifetime a picturesque river valley. Our 32,500-square-foot, slate-roofed, burgundy-colored, brick-and-sandstone-banded Education and Visitors Center will transform this expedient but inauspicious arrival into a varied and dramatic journey. Visitors will enter through a top-lighted great hall; off the hall are a shop, orientation galleries, small theater, and 176-seat lecture hall. They will then ascend to the second floor, on the level of Nook Farm, via a gently paced, skylighted stepped ramp wrapped around a two-thousand-square-foot exhibit gallery. At the top of the ramp, a light-filled café and divisible classroom open to a terrace where visitors will get their first glimpse of Twain's house. Tucked away on the third level are curatorial offices, a reading room, collection storage, and conservation facilities.

1

2

0 10 20   40 ft

3

0 30 60   120 ft

4

5

6

6. *Great hall at first
floor looking toward
orientation video
screening room*
7. *Great hall at second
floor looking toward
changing exhibit
gallery*
8. *Theater*

7

8

United States Courthouse

Richmond, Virginia
2001–2006

530   Located at the boundary between Richmond's historic commercial core, now being reinvented as a performing-arts district, and the Capitol Square district, this new federal courthouse sits among the important civic buildings lining Broad Street: City Hall, the State Assembly Building, and the State Library. The footprint of the 325,000-square-foot building is a bowed slab, intended to function as a corner post for the Capitol Square district, which the south-facing outer radius overlooks. The curving footprint provides a gardenlike setting for two adjacent historic churches, St. Peter's (1835, 1854) and St. Paul's (Thomas S. Stewart, 1845). On the north, cradled in the building's inner radius, a hundred-foot-high atrium turns a less formal face to the commercial district. Public galleries facing the atrium lead visitors to administrative offices on the lower four floors and nine courtrooms on the upper three. At night, the illuminated atrium and landscaped areas will provide a dramatic backdrop for the developing performing-arts district.

1. *Sixth-floor (courtroom level) plan*
2. *First-floor plan*
3. *Cutaway axonometric of entry sequence*
4. *Entry facade*
5. *Aerial view from Capitol Square*

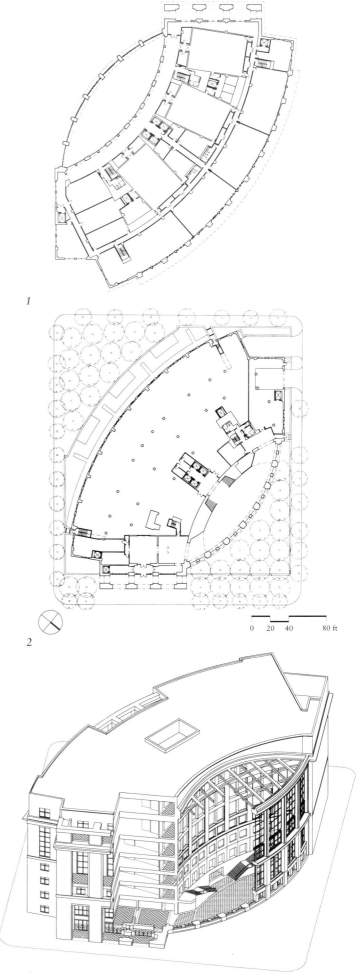

1

2

0 20 40   80 ft

3

4

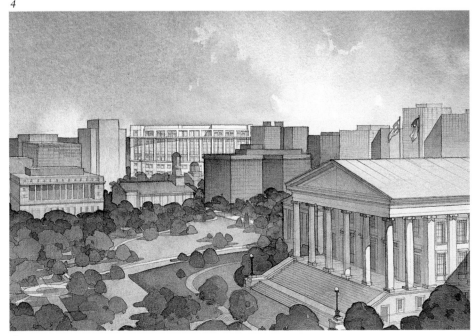

5

Torre Almirante

*Avenida Almirante Barroso
Rio de Janeiro, Brazil
2001–2004*

532 · A thirty-six-story, 550,000-square-foot office tower for international developer Hines, Torre Almirante will confront the intersection of Avenida Almirante Barroso and Avenida Aranha with a dramatically flared corner element, illuminated by continuously changing lighting displays from LED fixtures concealed within the curtain wall, that will become a beacon on the Rio skyline. The luminous glow of the lobby's twenty-foot-tall backlighted onyx wall will create a similar beacon at street level, visible from a double-height open-air loggia that forms a part of downtown Rio's system of continuous arcades. Above the ground floor, three stacked two-story winter gardens will further animate the corner by providing unique meeting spaces for tenants. The aluminum-frame curtain wall features high-performance blue-green glazing. Buff-colored Brazilian granite panels are interwoven to visually connect the base of the tower to neighboring masonry buildings.

1

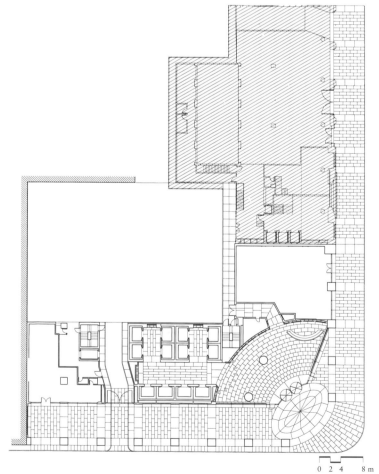

2

0 2 4   8 m

4. *Facade detail at corner*
5. *Facade detail at Avenida Arannha*
6. *Skyline view looking west from Guanabara Bay*

4

5

6

Jacksonville Public Library

Jacksonville, Florida
2001–2004

1. Conference
   center lobby
2. Site plan
3. Principal entry
   facade
4. Courtyard

536 The Jacksonville Public Library is intended to be an efficient, state-of-the-art facility that will also be a significant public place with intimate and grand rooms, garden courtyards, conference areas, cafés, and the like. Designed to attract the diverse community of Jacksonville, by virtue of its exterior forms and interior spaces it will become a destination without peer in the city.

Our proposal, selected in competition in 2001, reflects Jacksonville's tradition of civic buildings that speak in a classical language adapted to the local climate and culture. The new library will face Hemming Plaza with a generously proportioned main entrance that leads past a café and popular library to the entry hall and circulation desk. A monumental stair culminates at the hundred-foot-square, forty-six-foot-high, handkerchief-vaulted grand reading room. On the second floor, smaller reading areas for various departments are grouped around a planted courtyard and fountain.

1

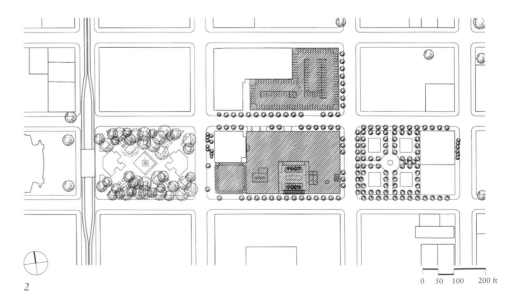

2

0   50   100   200 ft

3

4

5

5. Stair at
   ground floor
6. Section facing
   north
7. Stair at third
   floor
8. Lower-floor
   (conference
   center) plan
9. Second-floor
   plan

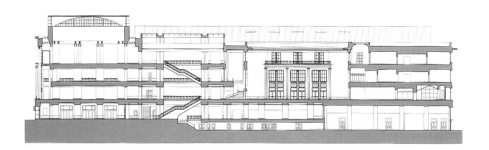

6

7

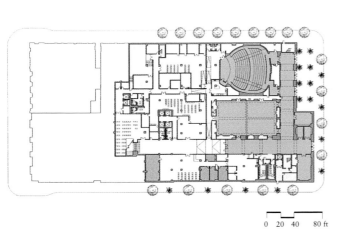

8

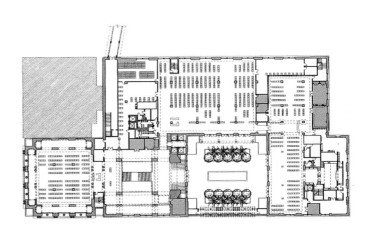

9

0 20 40   80 ft

10

10. *Special collections reading room*
11. *Children's reading room*
12. *Grand reading room*
13. *Teens' reading room*

11

12

13

The Plaza at PPL Center

Allentown, Pennsylvania
2001–2003

542   This new building represents the commitment of developer Liberty Property Trust and tenant PPL both to downtown Allentown and to environmentally sustainable design. The 287,000-square-foot, eight-story building sits on the north half of a full block site behind a public plaza; to the west, across North Ninth Street, is the historic Pennsylvania Power and Light Tower (Helmle, Corbett, and Harrison, 1928), which we consider an integral part of the composition. The site, formerly home to Hess Brothers department store, is envisioned as the western anchor of the Hamilton Street axis, a critical component of the master plan for Allentown's revitalization.

Within the building, the main double-height lobby and two secondary entrances converge on an eight-story, top-lighted atrium that provides a central point of orientation. In addition, two two-story south-facing winter gardens integrated into the office floors overlook the plaza. External sunshades on each floor of the south facade and a planted roof help reduce heat gain. The building's skin is composed of lightly tinted high-performance glass with silver-gray metal detailing and buff-colored precast-concrete spandrels; these materials significantly exceed current energy-performance standards.

At the top of the building a two-level trading room features raised flooring to accommodate cable distribution and energy-efficient air supply. A dramatically vaulted ceiling brings diffuse natural and artificial light deep into the space.

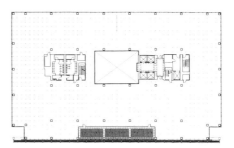

1

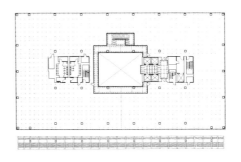

2

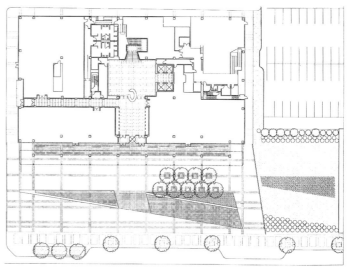

0 10 20   40 ft

3

4

5

6

One St. Thomas Street

Toronto, Ontario, Canada
2001–

1. *View from south-east to townhouses and base of tower*
2. *Site plan*
3. *View from south-west*

544 This twenty-nine-story, 250,000-square-foot apartment tower and its attached three-story townhouses comprise a total of one hundred condominium units. The project creates a transition between the high-rise residential buildings of Toronto's Bay Street and the low-rise residential buildings to the west. The pedestrian entrance to the tower is on Charles Street; the automobile drop-off and service access are located off a drive that wraps behind the tower. The narrow square tower rises through a series of setbacks to a sculptural penthouse and lantern that will create a recognizable profile on the Toronto skyline.

1

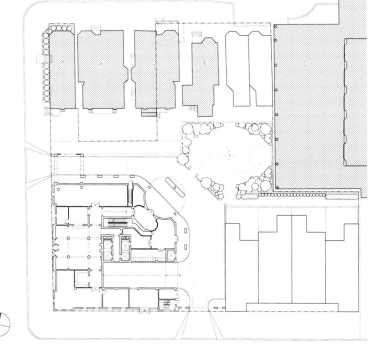

2

0 2.5 5   10 m

3

Smeal College of Business Administration
Pennsylvania State University

State College, Pennsylvania
2001–

546 At Penn State, working within the university's master plan, we have prepared design guidelines for six buildings in the new east subcampus. We are going ahead with designs for the 210,000-square-foot, four-story Smeal College of Business Administration and an adjacent 1,280-car garage and chiller plant. Intended to consolidate currently dispersed graduate and undergraduate business programs, the Smeal College building, together with the proposed School of Forestry, will form a bold crescent that defines the edge of the Meadow, a large sloping greensward that forms a gateway to a new north-south mall. The undergraduate and graduate programs of Smeal College are housed in two bar buildings that meet in a four-story glazed atrium with a sculptural stair that provides access to all levels and offers views across the Meadow to the mountains beyond.

1

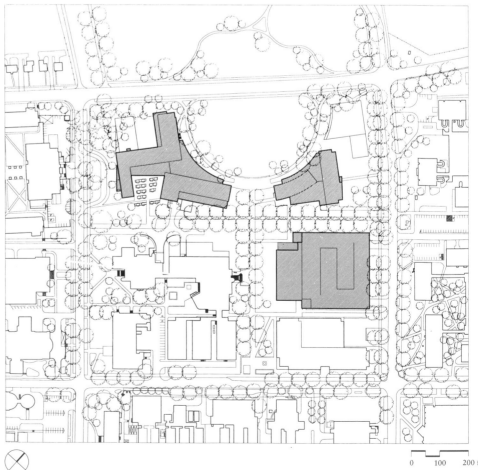

0 100 200 ft

2

1. Shortlidge Road
   facade
2. Site plan
3. View from the
   Meadow
4. Atrium
5. First-floor plan

547

3

4

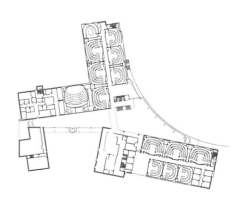

5

Philadelphia Naval
Business Center

Philadelphia, Pennsylvania
Competition, 2002

548   Located at the confluence of the Delaware and Schuylkill Rivers three and a half miles south of downtown Philadelphia, the thousand-acre Philadelphia Navy Yard contains a small but vibrant core of active Navy uses and a new shipbuilding facility adjacent to over six hundred acres of decommissioned land designated for redevelopment. Our clients were invited by the Philadelphia Industrial Development Corporation to submit a proposal for the planning and development of a sixty-acre office park, the Gateway Business Center, within the Navy Yard adjacent to the Broad Street entrance. Along with a design team of both Philadelphia-based and international consultants, we felt that Gateway Center could not be planned without a comprehensive look at the rest of the Navy Yard, and so our proposal considers all Navy Yard property along and to the east of Broad Street.

The plan proposes a 15-million-square-foot mixed-use community with approximately 1.5 million square feet of office space, 8,800 units of housing, and a combination of other commercial and recreational uses. A boulevard set at an angle to the street grid of the Navy Yard's historic core leads from the Broad Street entrance through a campus of three- to five-story office buildings to a new recreational marina. Surrounding the marina are a convention hotel, shops, and office and residential buildings. A series of districts, each with a distinct character, provides the vitality and balance needed for a lively urban center. To the west, buildings within the Navy Yard's core will be rehabilitated and reused, and vacant sites will be developed with townhouses and apartment buildings; to the north, a tax-incentive zone calls for light-industrial and research and development uses; to the east, a new residential district along a south-facing boardwalk and around two public squares will be served by a new public school and a recreation center. The PIDC selected our clients' development team for the Gateway Business Center and will work with us and them to refine the plan.

1

2

0 30 60 120 ft

1. Plan with existing
   conditions
2. Proposed site plan
3. Aerial view looking
   southeast
4. Aerial view of
   Gateway Circle

3

4

Meadowlands Master Plan

*Lyndhurst, Rutherford, and
North Arlington, New Jersey
2002–*

550 The three-thousand-acre brownfield site
for this mixed-use development in the
New Jersey Meadowlands includes six
separate landfill parcels. Located just over
eight miles west of midtown Manhattan,
the project calls for 1.2 million square
feet of office space; 650 hotel rooms;
1,500 residential units; 100,000 square
feet of retail; a conference center; and
36 holes of golf with two clubhouses
totaling 75,000 square feet. We will
collaborate on the master plan and also
provide conceptual designs for several
buildings, including the gateway hotel,
office buildings, resort hotel, clubhouses,
mixed-use apartment blocks, and stand-
alone retail.

1. Aerial view
2. Site plan
3. Location plan

1

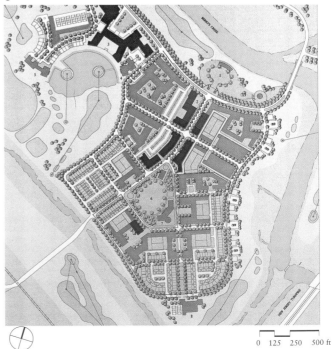

2

0 125 250 500 ft

3

Master Plan

Heiligendamm, Germany
2002–

1. Site plan
2. Aerial view
3. Golf club hotel
   from golf course

552 In 1996, we were commissioned to develop a preservation plan for Heiligendamm, one of Europe's oldest seaside resorts. Our second plan for the reinvention of Heiligendamm knits new development into the faded glory of the town. The design looks back to the English Regency precedents of the historic waterfront buildings that are being renovated as a luxury apartment hotel and conference center. A centrally located village green with restaurants and shops looks southwest over a new pond and golf course to distant farm fields. Main roads into the village converge on this green; a short distance to the east are a golf club and another hotel. Entry into the village from the west is through a market square conceived as an extension of existing retail and institutional development.

Residential neighborhoods are organized around a network of parks and a clear hierarchy of roads that encompasses everything from wide, gently curving boulevards to intimate winding residential streets. Small mixed-use and apartment buildings surround the market square and village green. Architectural guidelines for a variety of attached and detached single-family houses will ensure that new construction embraces and enhances the neoclassical character of the historic town.

1

0 10 20   40 m

553

2

3

Resort de Veneguera

*Gran Canaria, Canary Islands,
Spain
Competition, 2002*

554 The new town of Resort de Veneguera
will occupy one of the last undeveloped
sites on Gran Canaria, the largest of the
Canary Islands. The site, a ravine on the
southwest coast, is 1,200 feet wide at the
ocean and two miles deep. When
completed, the town will accommodate
sixteen thousand residents and visitors
in hotels, apartments, and single-family
houses. The downtown is organized
around a traditional Spanish *plaza mayor*,
the location of the main bus terminal.
The plaza is surrounded by hotels
incorporating ground-floor retail,
a market, and a six-screen movie theater.
Pedestrian ways lined with shops and
cafés lead to the beachfront promenade,
which curves gently along a beachside
park that incorporates various
recreational uses. To the north are
a marina and sporting harbor.

The main village is bisected by a grand
street that runs from a hotel at the top
of the hill all the way to the *plaza mayor*,
terminating in a staircase that steps down
to a waterfront plaza. The town is
organized into five residential neighborhoods, each with its own public park.
Each neighborhood is organized with
a street and block plan; blocks are
subdivided into smaller quadrants by
pedestrian paths that lead to the sea. Each
quadrant contains a mix of housing types
arranged around a shared pool court.
Ringing the top of the village are small
single-family villas. The main road into
town from the north passes through
a thirty-six-hole golf course; the golf
clubhouse at the top of the ravine looks
down over the village to the sea.

1

2

1. *Aerial view*
2. *Downtown detail plan
   at five meters above
   sea level*
3. *Downtown detail plan
   at ten meters above sea
   level*
4. *Downtown detail plan
   at thirty-five meters
   above sea level*

3

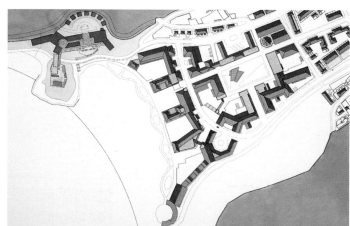

4

5. Plaza mayor
6. *Stair from beach to plaza mayor*
7. *Golf club*
8. *Courtyard residences*
9. *View from entry road*
10. *Beachside restaurant*

5

6

7

8

9

10

Additional Projects

Addition to House at Apaquogue
East Hampton, New York, 2000–2001

Seven years after we completed their house, our clients decided they needed additional space for guest quarters and an exercise room. The addition, at the south end of the house, completes the composition we had originally intended.

House Renovation
Bel Air, California, 2000–2001

A simple and symmetrical screen of new construction, with attenuated Ionic detailing, gives balance and coherence to a Regency-inspired house from the 1930s. Outdoor seating is sheltered by movable, sail-like canvas panels.

International Storytelling Center
Jonesborough, Tennessee, 1996–2002

Dedicated to the preservation and promulgation of oral storytelling, the National Storytelling Center is being realized in stages. Located at the edge of the most urban stretch of Main Street in Tennessee's best-preserved town, where it forms a courtyard with the historic Chester Inn, the new building makes its own distinct statement, announcing itself on the skyline with a fifty-foot tower.

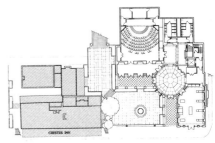

Santa Monica UCLA Medical Center/ Orthopaedic Hospital Replacement Project
Santa Monica, California, 1997–2007

After Santa Monica Hospital was damaged in the 1994 Northridge earthquake, the UCLA Health System acquired the facility. The new center, which will also include a new Orthopaedic Hospital, will face Wilshire Boulevard with a major tower and park. Brick, terra-cotta, and stone courtyards, plazas, and gardens visually connect this facility with the main UCLA campus.

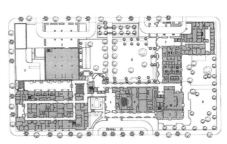

Yonkers Public Library and Board of Education Offices
Yonkers, New York, 1998

This design transforms a derelict 130,000-square-foot industrial building into an information-age structure that remembers its roots. We proposed a 60,000-square-foot addition that would have organized the library and the Board of Education offices in separate "towers," providing each with spectacular river views.

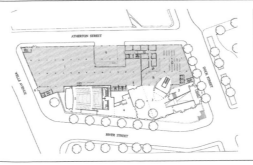

Accessories
Valli & Valli, 1998–2002

This collection of bathroom accessories and door levers complements the modern classicism of our residential architecture.

Residence in Forest Hill
Toronto, Ontario, 1998

This compact house with rough stone and split-board exterior, slate roofs, and bracketed porches was intended to complement neighboring houses in an established suburb. To bring as much light into the house as possible, the main rooms are located to one side of the deep, narrow site, taking advantage of the land's natural slope. A series of terraced lawns descends from the main structure to the swimming pool below.

Morris Quadrangle, Corporate Campus
Florham Park, New Jersey, 1998–

Seven office buildings are planned to provide 800,000 square feet of space on three sites on a 180-acre wooded property. Four four-story, 133,000-square-foot classically inspired buildings connected by screen walls will surround a landscaped courtyard. Two 110,000-square-foot buildings to the south will have prominent exposure to the Columbia Turnpike, and a one-story building to the north is designed for research and development.

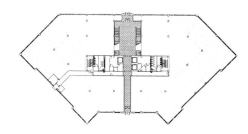 

Addition to Enron Corporate Headquarters
Houston, Texas, Competition, 1998

A competition design for a new office tower across from the fifteen-year-old Enron headquarters incorporated a 220-foot daylighted trading room, corporate conference center, employee restaurant, and fitness center into the first three floors of the distinctly shaped building.

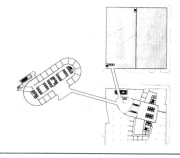 

425 Fifth Avenue
New York, New York, 1998

This sixty-three-story mixed-use tower was designed to be cantilevered over an adjoining five-story building. At street level, an adjacent plaza on Thirty-eighth Street was intended both as a landscaped backdrop for the building's residential lobby and as a tranquil garden for local residents. We withdrew from the project in 2000.

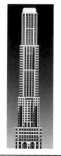 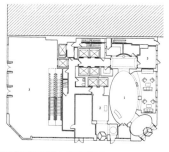 

311 Bay Street
Toronto, Canada, 1998

This thirty-story building at the heart of Toronto's business and financial district comprised three distinct elements: a base of retail and hotel amenities, a shaft containing 262 hotel rooms, and a stepped top housing fifty-six apartments. The red-brick tower facade is modulated with fluted cast-stone pilasters and cornices that evoke North America's grand urban hotels of the 1920s and 1930s.

Performing Arts Center
Proctor Academy, Andover, New Hampshire, 1998

This thirty-four-thousand-square-foot building for a New England boarding school was to contain a 450-seat proscenium theater, one-thousand-square-foot black-box performance space, dance studio, recording studio, and recital space. Carpenter-classical white clapboard walls and painted wood windows rest on a stone base and rise to a copper roof, suggesting a barn or meetinghouse converted to a theater.

Wave Hill Chair
Riverdale, The Bronx, New York, 2000

For Wave Hill's Annual Spring Gala Silent Auction Benefit, we reimagined the garden chair in mirror to reflect the natural beauty of Wave Hill's landscape.

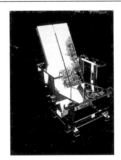

Meetinghouse Golf Club
Edgartown, Martha's Vineyard, Massachusetts, 1998

Familiar elements and materials such as porches, dormers, columns, and shingles combine with a floor plan that turns to take advantage of the topography and views of the Edgartown Great Pond.

Gingerbread House for
the *New York Times Magazine*
1998

Typical gingerbread houses are generic decorated boxes; this one, designed in collaboration with pastry chef Jacques Torres, is more considered. The Shingle-style cottage appeals to the imagination as well as to the appetite and evokes memories—real or imagined—of holidays long past.

Broad Center for the Biological Sciences
California Institute of Technology,
Pasadena, California, Competition, 1998

For a three-story research building at the northwest corner of the historic Caltech campus we proposed a board-formed concrete building trimmed with cast stone, and articulated to continue the line of formal exploration begun at Caltech by Bertram Goodhue, Gordon Kaufman, and Myron Hunt.

 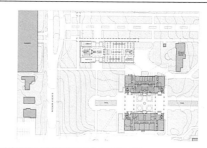

Presidio Village
San Francisco, California, Competition, 1998

By congressional mandate, the Presidio Trust was given responsibility for guiding the transformation of Presidio Park into a self-sustaining portion of the Golden Gate National Recreational Area. Our design for the Letterman site proposed office, residential, and retail space in a grid plan around a central green.

55 East Erie
Chicago, Illinois, 1999

This eighty-four-story, 920-foot-high mixed-use building planned for half a city block in Chicago's historic Mansion District was intended to celebrate height in a manner characteristic of Chicago's prewar skyline.

 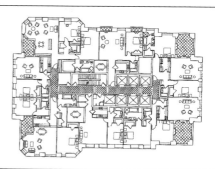

Residence
Pacific Palisades, California, 1999

Inspired by the vernacular *poderis* of Tuscany and Umbria, the pavilions and dependencies that make up this house are organized loosely around a water court that brings natural light into each pavilion. The principal rooms are oriented outward on three sides to give shaded garden views through loggias, pergolas, and broad overhanging eaves.

De Taats
Utrecht, The Netherlands, 1999–

Connecting the new Papendorp development to the city of Utrecht across the Amsterdam-Rhine Canal, De Taats will consist of seven buildings, four atrium spaces surrounding a courtyard, and a central service area. Six eight-story buildings form urban walls along Westlaan and Oostlaan, and a seventeen-story building at the northern end of the block punctuates the skyline.

 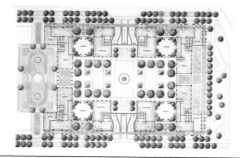 

House Renovation
San Francisco, California, 1999–2000

While respecting the integrity of the original architecture both inside and out, the renovation of this townhouse of about 1909 adds such amenities as a modern kitchen and a master bedroom suite to a plan that has changed little in more than ninety years. Most significant, the main-level rooms now open to a new private garden.

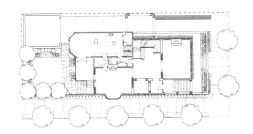

Disney's Beach Club Villas
Walt Disney World Resort,
Lake Buena Vista, Florida, 1999–2002

The Beach Club Villas are an addition to our Beach Club Resort Hotel (1991), which echoed Stick-style mid-Atlantic beach resorts such as Cape May, New Jersey. The existing blue hotel is at the classical end of the Stick-style spectrum; the new green villas, with their thin pointed arches, are at the Gothic end. White-painted wood arches, brackets, and lattice provide a changing show of light and shadow.

Apartment in the Chatham
New York, New York, 1999–2001

This New York pied-à-terre is similar in its detailing and muted colors to a residence we designed for the same couple on the West Coast.

House and Guest Cottage
Sonoma County, California, 1999–

The main house will nestle between live oaks and a meadow, oriented south to Sonoma Mountain. The guest cottage will occupy the prow of a hill to the northwest, with views over an olive grove east toward the Napa Valley. Simple metal gable shed roofs with stone piers and board-and-batten siding recall the rustic vernacular of Sonoma Valley.

Residence
Woodside, California, 1999

This new house and related facilities were organized according to a relaxed but carefully orchestrated strategy that recalls Sir Edwin Lutyens's Grey Walls. We took advantage of a site that includes century-old live oaks, an open meadow, and a recently completed guest house and stable, while satisfying complex zoning constraints, unusual easement and right-of-way requirements, and a fixed entrance location.

Guest Cottage at Siansconset
Nantucket, Massachusetts, 1999–

This symmetrically massed outbuilding counterpoints a rambling, century-old, Shingle-style summer residence.

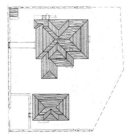

Residence
San Francisco, California, 1999–

To take advantage of a steeply sloping lot that offers superb views north to San Francisco Bay and east to the city's only vineyard and simultaneously to respond to the concerns of neighbors anxious to protect their own views, we proposed an L-shaped house that creates a wide courtyard. The narrow face of the L fronts the street, where its two-story facade is similar in scale to neighboring houses.

Emily Howe Memorial Library
Hanover, New Hampshire, 1999–

This project doubles the size of the thirty-year-old Howe Library with a wing that will provide badly needed community meeting space, expanded services for children and teenagers, a gallery, and significant new infrastructure for computer and communication services. By relocating existing parking, our design also creates new outdoor spaces—including an amphitheater and an area for children—and more strongly identifies the library as a public institution.

Residence at Squibnocket
Chilmark, Martha's Vineyard, Massachusetts, 1999

This low-slung shingled house was designed to fit the gentle topography of its meadow site.

Residence
Westport, Connecticut, 1999–

This new six-thousand-square-foot Shingle-style house was designed for a hilltop site in Westport with panoramic views of the Long Island Sound.

Colorado Christian University
Lakewood, Colorado, Competition, 1999

For the university's new campus, on a gently sloping saddle at the top of an open valley, we proposed a compact pedestrian-oriented plan with a quadrangle framed on three sides by a chapel, a library, and an arts center and open on the fourth side to western views. The principal academic buildings are positioned along a pedestrian walkway and form secondary quadrangles that are oriented to take advantage of sunlight and vistas.

Campus Center
Indiana University/Purdue University, Indianapolis, Indiana, 2000

Our design for a campus center at the intersection of two campus grid systems organizes computer rooms, food services, retail facilities, counseling services, a two-hundred-seat theater, and a fifty-thousand-square-foot conference center around a skylighted atrium. Glassy facades contrast with neighboring brick and limestone buildings.

Tuhaye
Park City, Utah, 2001–

For a new community located near Park City, Utah, we designed a golf clubhouse and health club, both arranged on sloping sites to take advantage of spectacular views to the Jordanelle Reservoir and the mountains beyond.

Residence on Maui
Kapalua, Hawaii, 1999

Composed as a series of descending terraces and pavilions on the slopes of the Honolulu ridge, this house opens to striking views of the Pacific and the islands of Molokai and Lanai. A steep winding drive, high-walled motor court, and entrance loggia bridging a pond create a dramatic entrance sequence; inside, living spaces are casually grouped around garden and pool terraces that punctuate the landscape.

School of Business
College of William and Mary, Williamsburg, Virginia, 1999–

The proposed new home for the School of Business at the College of William and Mary consists of a 160,000-square-foot H-plan building that forms a gateway between the present campus to the west and the Colgate Darden gardens and Lake Matoaka amphitheater to the east.

Residence
Fort Washington, Pennsylvania,
2000

The design for this house echoes the sprawling, low-profile stone farmhouses common to the area while responding to mature landscape features on the rolling site.

UCLA Cancer Center
Westwood Campus, University of California,
Los Angeles, California, 2000

The 407,000-square-foot cancer center maintains the separate identities of its three components—treatment center, research laboratories, and outpatient facilities—while creating a collegial atmosphere for clinicians and researchers. Located at the gateway between UCLA and the adjacent Westwood Village, the center reestablishes the courtyard tradition and Northern Italianate architectural style that characterize the heart of the campus.

Residence
Ross, California, 2000–

Our initial scheme proposed a modest house with simple gabled and shed-roofed elements composed in the manner of Italian hill-town houses that have been added to over time. The dominant chimney of our second scheme—inspired by the informal yet tautly configured shingled cottages of Wilson Eyre and Ernest Coxhead—embodies a more iconic representation of hearth and home.

"Udderly Delightful"
Cow Parade, West Orange, New Jersey, 2000

In the summer of 2000, West Orange, New Jersey, sponsored a cow parade in which artists and architects were asked to decorate prefabricated fiberglass cows for public locations around the city. Invited by the West Orange Public Library to adopt a cow, we used plastic, wood, metal, paint, and gold leaf to fashion a Jersey cow howdah.

 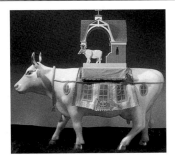

Snowmass Base Village
Snowmass, Colorado, Competition, 2000

Our design for Snowmass Base Village organizes various buildings around three distinct courtyards. The Day Lodge defines the edge of the village square while a major hotel shapes a south-facing courtyard, giving the restaurants, solarium, pool, and skating rink a view of the slopes. To the east, a park forms the heart of a residential neighborhood.

Pequot Library
Southport, Connecticut, 2000

The original Pequot Library, designed by R. H. Robertson in a Romanesque Revival style, included a vaulted reading room and an auditorium with stained-glass clerestory windows. Our proposed addition, to replace one from the 1970s, wraps two wings and a gallery around a new courtyard and restores the original building as reading rooms and collection storage.

Town Center, DC Ranch
Scottsdale, Arizona, 2000

For the Town Center, a new development in the high Sonoran Desert at the edge of Scottsdale, Arizona, we planned streets and paths, grand squares, and intimate walkways in relation to views, especially the vista to the site's principal feature, a picturesque desert wash. Walking will be encouraged, but the reality of the automobile is recognized in parking structures tucked away in the centers of the blocks.

55 Railroad Avenue
Greenwich, Connecticut, 2000–2003

In an effort to reposition a visually uninteresting but strategically located office property, we added a cantilevered glass-and-steel canopy, redesigned the lobby, and transformed a sunken concrete plaza into a garden with outdoor tables and chairs set between a bosque of flowering trees, a raised panel of turf, and an eighty-foot-long water wall.

Campus Center
College of Notre Dame of Maryland, Baltimore, Maryland, 2000

The proposed ninety-thousand-square-foot campus center steps down a hillside to connect administrative and indoor athletic facilities above with playing fields and parking below. The center includes a 500-seat dining hall with north-facing bay windows, a 185-seat lecture room with adjoining classrooms, and offices for student services, all wrapped around an existing gymnasium to mask its blank facade.

 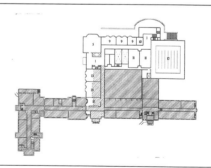

Townhouses on Liberty Street
Frisco Square, Frisco, Texas, 2000–2004

Frisco Square, a new residential community near Dallas, Texas, was planned by David Schwarz. We designed a block of eight townhouses, each with its own individual expression, to form one coherent composition.

Apartment Building for Parcel 19B
Battery Park City, New York, New York,
2000–

This twenty-five-story, 264-unit, stone-trimmed, red-brick apartment tower was designed in response to the Battery Park City Authority's mandate for sustainable architecture.

Office Building
Centre du Val d'Europe, Marne-la-Vallée,
France, 2000–

The curved colonnaded front and tower of this six-story building define the entry to the new town of Val d'Europe. At the rear, the building steps down to face a residential development across a courtyard. Details are rendered in stucco and stone.

Master Plan and Student Center
Hopkins School, New Haven, Connecticut,
2000

This thirty-thousand-square-foot student center, which provides a 350-seat dining hall, is one component in a master plan that proposes new buildings in character with the Hopkins School's existing Georgian brick vocabulary.

Folie Bergère
Parrish Art Museum exhibition "Follies:
Fantasy in the Landscape," 2001

Our contribution to the exhibition depicted a colossal Louis XV bergère reimagined as a lattice garden pavilion for an overachieving Southampton garden party.

Cottage
Carmel, California, 2001–

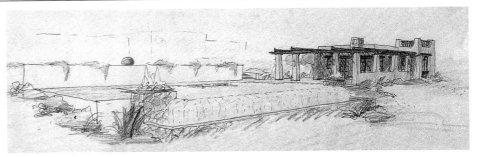

Set below an existing Southwestern-style house on the crest of the hills east of Carmel, this cottage will help screen midground views of nearby development that mar the scene of distant vineyards and coastline ridges.

Simons Center for the Arts
College of Charleston, Charleston,
South Carolina, 2001–

The Simons Center is a thirty-year-old facility housing
the art, music, theater, and art history departments at
the College of Charleston. In addition to renovating
existing building, our design will include a thirty-
thousand-square-foot addition. We undertook the
project with the intention of uniting the center with
the historic character of the college's architecture.

Residence at One Central Park
New York, New York, 2001

Our sketch design, prepared for the developer,
demonstrates how the seventy-fifth floor of a
dramatically shaped, glass-sheathed tower now under
construction could be arranged to suggest the figural
spaces of New York's grand apartments.

Residence on Sunset Boulevard
Beverly Hills, California, 2001

This house, an Italianate villa in a park, is carefully
sited on its prominent corner lot to offer long garden
views from the principal rooms. A central courtyard
ringed by a glazed arcade allows a compact and logi-
cal arrangement of rooms.

Columbus Seniors Center
Columbus, Indiana, 2001–

Located in Mill Race Park, within walking distance
of downtown, the thirty-thousand-square-foot Seniors
Center is intended to feel like a big house rather than
a small institution. The one-story buff-brick and
Indiana-limestone building provides meeting, dining,
craft, and fitness and health facilities in wings that
separate the programs by function and create sun
exposure for most rooms from two or three sides.

Apartment Building
Larchmont, New York, 2002–

Echoing the massing and character of much-admired
nearby apartment buildings from the 1920s, this
185-unit, 140,000-square-foot apartment building
will include a small retail center and landscaped
open space.

Residence at Hubbard's Woods
Winnetka, Illinois, 2002–

Located on one of Winnetka's few remaining undivided estate lots, this house—inspired by the free eclecticism of architects such as Howard Van Doren Shaw and David Adler—combines English and American elements into a linear composition that respects existing plantings and maximizes lake views to the east while introducing south light into most rooms.

Residence on Bel Air Road
Los Angeles, California, 2002–

The mass of this stone-clad house is resolved into discrete and semi-independent pavilions that create a sequence of walled courtyards and open lawns.

Baker Library Academic Center
Harvard Business School, Boston, Massachusetts, 2002–2005

By removing the un-air-conditioned structural stacks at the back of Baker Library, the centerpiece of McKim, Mead & White's master plan for the Harvard Business School campus, our design will create offices for faculty, provide a new skylighted path to the restored reading room, and allow circulation through the building from the existing north portico to a new entry at the building's new south front.

Project Information

572 **Residence**
Chestnut Hill, Massachusetts, 1986–1991

Associate Partners: Armand LeGardeur, Charles Warren. Senior Assistant: Mark Johnson. Assistants: Thomas Gay, Laurie Kerr, Elizabeth Kozarec, Rosamund Young. Interiors Associate: Raúl Morillas. Interiors Assistants: Patricia Burns, Stephan Johnson, Sharon Pett.

Robert A. M. Stern, "Design as Emulation," *Architectural Design*, September/October 1988, 20–27.

The American Houses of Robert A. M. Stern, introduction by Clive Aslet (New York: Rizzoli, 1991), 56–61.

Felicia Paik, "Private Properties: Architectural Artistry," *Wall Street Journal*, July 17, 1998, W:8.

Felicia Paik and Rebecca Lowell, "Private Properties," *Wall Street Journal*, May 21, 1999, W:12.

Gap Inc. Offices at Two Folsom Street
San Francisco, California, 1992–2001

Partner: Graham S. Wyatt. Project Designers: Gregory Christopher, Edwin Hofmann, Michael Jones, Lee Ledbetter. Assistants: Dennis Giobbe, Haven Knight, Antonio Ng, Anthony Polito, Michael Wilbur. Associate Architect: Gensler.

Gerald D. Adams, "N.Y. Architect Firm Gets the Gap Plum," *San Francisco Examiner*, December 2, 1992, C:1, 5.

"Business Briefs: Gap Picks Designer for Headquarters," *San Francisco Chronicle*, December 2, 1992, C:2.

"Details," *Architecture*, January 1993, 22.

"Details," *Architecture*, November 1994, 29.

Dan Levy, "Gap Wins OK for Site at S.F. Embarcadero," *San Francisco Chronicle*, January 11, 1995, A:20.

John King, "Filling an Architectural Gap," *San Francisco Chronicle*, January 20, 1997, B:1–4.

Jason B. Johnson, "Bid to Stop Gap Project Is Defeated," *San Francisco Chronicle*, September 2, 1998, A:13, 18.

Robert A. M. Stern: Buildings and Projects, 1993–1998 (New York: The Monacelli Press, 1998), 132–35.

Martin Holden, "SoMa Rising," *San Francisco*, February 2001, 50–63.

Charlie Ryrie, "Breaking New Ground," *Gardens Illustrated*, May 2001, 20–21.

John King, "Fall into Gap of Mediocrity: Chain Headquarters' New Embarcadero Building Disappoints," *San Francisco Chronicle*, June 11, 2001, A:1, 11.

John King, "Starchitecture: Why Does the Bay Area Confound the Best Architects?" *San Francisco Chronicle Magazine*, October 27, 2002, 12–17.

Residence
Kings Point, New York, 1992–1997

Partner: Roger H. Seifter. Associate: John Berson. Senior Assistant: Robert Epley. Assistants: Jason Depierre, Amy Farber, Michael Levendusky. Landscape Associate: Brian Sawyer. Landscape Project Manager: Charlotte Frieze. Interiors Associate: Patricia Burns Ross. Interior Designer: Mark Hampton. Interiors Assistant: Claire Ratliff.

Robert A. M. Stern: Buildings and Projects, 1993–1998 (New York: The Monacelli Press, 1998), 136–37.

Moore Psychology Building, Dartmouth College
Hanover, New Hampshire, 1992–1999

Partner: Graham S. Wyatt. Project Architect: Preston Gumberich. Associates: Adam Anuszkiewicz, Augusta Barone. Senior Assistant: Meghan McDermott. Assistants: Elizabeth Adams, Ricardo Alvarez-Diaz, Frank de Santis, Shannon Gallagher, Jonas Goldberg, Claudia Lin, Quincey Nixon, Richard Schneider. Interiors Assistants: Peter Fleming, Damion Phillips, Claire Ratliff.

"New Psych Building Due in '99," *Dartmouth Life*, June 1997, 1–2.

Robert A. M. Stern: Buildings and Projects, 1993–1998 (New York: The Monacelli Press, 1998), 176–77.

North Campus Master Plan, Dartmouth College
Hanover, New Hampshire, Competition, 2001

Partner: Graham S. Wyatt. Senior Associate: Preston Gumberich. Assistants: Fred Berthelot, Jennifer Rice, Dennis Sagiev.

James McCown, "Dartmouth Looks to the Future: A Modern Plan for an Ivy League Campus," *Competitions*, Fall 2001, 32–41.

Residence in Preston Hollow
Dallas, Texas, 1993–2000

Associate Partner: Armand LeGardeur. Senior Assistants: Douglas Wright, Susi Yu. Assistants: Fred Berthelot, Diane Boston, Cristiana Gallo. Interiors Associate: Raúl Morillas. Interiors Assistants: Yi Liu Krooss, Claire Ratliff, Cynthia Tai, Joy Tucci. Landscape Associate: Brian Sawyer. Landscape Assistants: Laura Hynes, Marie Andree Soundy, Allison Towne, Mei Wu.

Robert A. M. Stern: Buildings and Projects, 1993–1998 (New York: The Monacelli Press, 1998), 190–91.

Residence in Montecito
Santa Barbara, California, 1993–1999

Partner: Roger H. Seifter. Associate: John Berson. Assistants: Jamie Alexander, Joseph Andriola, Joel Barkley, Amy Farber, Anselm Fusco, Michael Jacobs, Victor Jones, Lisa Shire. Landscape Associates: Robert Ermerins, Charlotte Frieze, Brian Sawyer, Ann Stokes. Interior Designer: Mariette Himes Gomez.

Robert A. M. Stern: Buildings and Projects, 1993–1998 (New York: The Monacelli Press, 1998), 206–9.

Mary McNamara, "Oprah's Garden Party," *O: The Oprah Magazine*, August 2002, 144–51.

Residence at North York
Toronto, Ontario, Canada, 1993–1998

Partner: Roger H. Seifter. Associate: Daniel Lobitz. Senior Assistant: Monique Agnew. Assistants: John Gilmer, Michael Levendusky, Renan Pierre. Landscape Associate: Brian Sawyer. Landscape Senior Assistant: Sarah Newbery. Landscape Assistant: Janell Denler. Interior Designer: Katherine Newman Design.

The American Houses of Robert A. M. Stern, introduction by Clive Aslet (New York: Rizzoli, 1991), 216–19.

Robert A. M. Stern: Buildings and Projects, 1987–1992, introduction by Vincent Scully (New York: Rizzoli, 1992), 310–11.

Robert A. M. Stern: Buildings and Projects, 1993–1998 (New York: The Monacelli Press, 1998), 210–11.

Mildred Schmertz, "Written in Stone," *Architectural Digest*, March 2002, 112–19, 190, 196.

Smith Campus Center, Pomona College

Claremont, California, 1993–1999

Partner: Graham S. Wyatt. Project Architect, Design: Adam Anuszkiewicz. Project Architect, Construction: Diane Scott-Burkin. Senior Assistant: John Cays. Assistants: Hernán Chebar, Tonia Long, Lenore Passavanti. Interiors Assistants: Damion Phillips, Chris Powell, Cynthia Tai.

Richard P. Dober, *Campus Architecture: Building in the Groves of Academe* (New York: McGraw-Hill, 1996), 181.

Robert A. M. Stern: Buildings and Projects, 1993–1998 (New York: The Monacelli Press, 1998), 212–13.

Patt Diroll, "A Building for the Future," *Pasadena Star News*, September 25, 1999, D:3.

"What's New at Pomona College: Pomona College Unveils New Campus Center," *Pomona College Magazine*, December 1999, online edition.

Lawrence Biemiller, "The Center of the Campus," *Pomona College Magazine*, Spring 2000, 38–43.

Susan Doubilet, "Smith Campus Center," *Architectural Record*, August 2000, 142–45.

National Advocacy Center

Columbia, South Carolina, 1993–1998

Partner: Graham S. Wyatt. Project Architect: Gary Brewer. Associate: Diane Scott-Burkin. Assistants: Kathy Pacchiana, Daniel Parolek, Jennifer Wlock, Youngmin Woo, Paul Zamek. Interiors Senior Assistant: Patricia Burns Ross. Landscape Senior Assistant: Ann Stokes. Associate Architect: HNTB. Local Architect: Wilson-Tate Architects, Inc.

Ann C. Sullivan, "Improving EIFS Performance," *Architecture*, May 1996, 251–53.

Clif LeBlanc, "Reno Wants Center to Fight Digital Crime," *The State* (Columbia, South Carolina), June 2, 1998, A:1, 6.

Robert A. M. Stern: Buildings and Projects, 1993–1998 (New York: The Monacelli Press, 1998), 214–15.

Chris Horn and Robert Clark, *University of South Carolina: A Portrait* (Columbia: South Carolina Press, 2001), 28–29, 42–43.

Residence in Pacific Heights

San Francisco, California, 1994–1999

Partner: Grant F. Marani. Associate: Elizabeth Kozarec. Senior Assistant: Katherine Oudens. Assistant: Johnny Cruz. Interior Designer: Agnes Bourne Studio with Geoffrey De Sousa.

Robert A. M. Stern: Buildings and Projects, 1993–1998 (New York: The Monacelli Press, 1998), 228–29.

Joan Chatfield-Taylor, "Living with Antiques: History by Design, Three Homes by Geoffrey De Sousa," *San Francisco*, November 1999, 7–19.

Patricia Leigh Brown, "Shingle Style by the Bay," *Architectural Digest*, November 2001, 18, 252–57, 315.

Sam Monahan, letter to the editor, *Architectural Digest*, January 2002, 18.

Beckley, West Virginia, 1994–1999

Partner: Grant F. Marani. Associate: Elizabeth Kozarec. Senior Assistant: John Gilmer. Assistants: Lindsay Bierman, Krystyan Keck, Dino Marcantonio, Kim Neuscheler, Daniel Parolek, Timothy Slattery. Interiors Senior Assistant: Scott Sloat. Landscape Associate: Ann Stokes. Landscape Senior Assistant: Sarah Newbery. Associate Architect: Einhorn Yaffee Prescott. Local Architect: SEM Partners.

Michael Wise, "Courthouses on Trial," *Metropolis*, May 1995, 100.

"GSA Design Excellence in Action," *AIArchitect*, mid-October 1995, 10.

"Federal Design Excellence," *Architecture*, January 1996, 60–95.

Edward Gunts, "Federal Courthouse Competition," *Architecture*, January 1996, 105–9.

Robert A. M. Stern: Buildings and Projects, 1993–1998 (New York: The Monacelli Press, 1998), 230–33.

Chris Stirewalt, "Verdict In on Federal Courthouses," *Charleston Daily Mail*, September 23, 1999, online edition.

Robert C. Byrd United States Courthouse and Federal Building, Beckley, West Virginia (Washington, D.C.: General Services Administration, 2000).

Lawrence Speck, "Robert C. Byrd United States Courthouse and Federal Building, Beckley, West Virginia," *Architecture*, January 2001, 17, 65, 71, 75–77, 102–9.

Vision + Voice: Design Excellence in Federal Architecture: Building Legacy (Washington, D.C.: General Services Administration, 2002), 50–52.

Residence and Guest House

Southampton, New York, 1994–1997

Associate Partner: Randy M. Correll. Senior Assistant: Geoffrey Mouen. Assistant: Timothy Slattery. Landscape Associate: Charlotte Frieze.

Robert A. M. Stern: Buildings and Projects, 1993–1998 (New York: The Monacelli Press, 1998), 240–41.

Tribeca Park

400 Chambers Street, Battery Park City, New York, New York, 1995–1999

Associate Partner: Barry Rice. Project Associate: Michael Jones. Assistants: John Ellis, Shannon Gallagher, Christine Kelley, Damion Phillips. Associate Architect: Costas Kondylis & Partners.

"HRH Building Tribeca Park," *New York Construction News*, June 1, 1998, 13.

Robert A. M. Stern: Buildings and Projects, 1993–1998 (New York: The Monacelli Press, 1998), 292–95.

Kate Kelly, "Building Boom of 1999: Will Manhattan Change into Tacky Condo Town?" *New York Observer*, February 1, 1999, 1, 11.

David W. Dunlap, "Filling In the Blanks at Battery Park City," *New York Times*, February 7, 1999, 11:1, 22.

Jo B. Hoffman, "The Neighborhood Guide: Financial District," *New York*, April 12, 1999.

Alexandra Lange, "The Towers that Will Be," *New York*, April 12, 1999, 42–44.

Rachelle Garbarine, "Luxury Condominiums Seeing Strong Demand," *New York Times*, April 16, 1999, B:9.

Jane Merkel, "Home, Sweet Home?" *Oculus*, September 1999, 12–13.

574   Trish Hall, "Former Navy Man Finds a Home by the River," *New York Times*, October 31, 1999, 11:2.

Norval White and Elliot Willensky, *AIA Guide to New York City*, 4th ed. (New York: Three Rivers Press, 2000), 51.

Deborah Baldwin, "The Humble Colossi of a Proud Cityscape," *New York Times*, January 18, 2001, F:10

"The Related Companies: A Mini Conglomerate," *New York Living*, May 2001, 54–55.

Francis Morrone, "Abroad in New York," *New York Sun*, August 16–18, 2002, 11.

Edison Field

Anaheim, California, 1995–1998

Partner: Paul L. Whalen. Associate Partner: Barry Rice. Senior Assistants: John Gilmer, Howard Shen. Assistants: Kyo Bannai, Molly Denver, Kurt Glauber, Edwin Hofmann, Christine Kelley, Julia Nelson, Daniel Parolek, Dennis Sagiev, David Solomon, Paul Zamek. Associate Architect: HOK Sport.

"Disney Park to Celebrate California," *New York Times*, July 15, 1996, D:2.

Marla Jo Fisher, "Architecture: Renovated Stadium Is a Product of Disney Whimsy and Baseball Tradition," *Orange County Register*, March 26, 1998, G:2.

J. A. Adande, "The Angels Get a Little Slice of Heaven," *Los Angeles Times*, March 28, 1998, A:1, 30.

John W. Swanson, "New-Look Stadium Premieres," *Anaheim Bulletin*, April 2, 1998, 1.

Rick Reiff and Nidal Ibrahim, "Edison International Field of Anaheim," *Orange County Business Journal*, April 6, 1998.

Roger Teffi, "Dream Team: How Architects, Designers, Imagineers Built Edison Field," *Orange County Business Journal*, April 13, 1998, 1, 17–18.

Warren Chiara, "Who's on Deck?" *New York Construction News*, July 1998, 27–32.

Robert A. M. Stern: Buildings and Projects, 1993–1998 (New York: The Monacelli Press, 1998), 296–99.

John E. Czarnecki, "Disney Strengthens Anaheim Presence with Planning and Pixie Dust," *Architectural Record*, April 2001, 49–52.

Residence

Kiawah Island, South Carolina, 1995–2003

Partner: Roger H. Seifter. Associate: Victoria Baran. Project Manager: Monique Agnew. Senior Assistant: Glenn Albrecht. Assistant: Tom Hickey. Landscape Associate: Marsh Kriplen. Landscape Senior Assistant: Ashley Christopher.

Robert A. M. Stern: Buildings and Projects, 1993–1998 (New York: The Monacelli Press, 1998), 302–3.

Disney Ambassador Hotel, Tokyo Disney Resort

Urayasu-shi, Chiba-ken, Japan, 1996–2000

Partner: Paul L. Whalen. Associate: John Gilmer. Assistants: Hernán Chebar, Shannon Gallagher, Allison Karn, David Solomon. Associate Architect: Nikken Sekkei Architects.

Robert A. M. Stern: Buildings and Projects, 1993–1998 (New York: The Monacelli Press, 1998), 304–5.

Shotenkenchiku, September 2000, 87–95.

Patricia Leigh Brown, "Tokyo's Disney Ambassador Hotel: Robert A. M. Stern Conjures a Moderne Fantasy for Japan's Magic Kingdom," *Architectural Digest*, August 2001, 32, 34, 36, 38.

Residential Quadrangle and Leo J. O'Donovan Central Dining Facility, Georgetown University

Washington, D.C., 1996–2003

Partner: Graham S. Wyatt. Project Designers: Frank de Santis, Jonilla Dorsten, Dana Gulling, Kevin O'Connor. Assistants: Marina Berendeeva, Edwin Hofmann, James Johnson, Antonio Ng, James Park, Jong-Hyuck Park, Lenore Passavanti, Katherine Snow, Karina Tengberg, Michael Wilbur, Yuri Zagorin, Paul Zamek. Landscape Associate: Dawn Handler. Landscape Assistants: Peter Arato, Norbert Holter, John Merritt, Eric Samuels. Interiors Associate: John Gilmer. Interiors Assistant: Paola Velazquez. Associate Architect: Einhorn Yaffee Prescott.

David Montgomery, "Georgetown Plans Complex with 800-Bed Dormitory," *Washington Post*, February 28, 1998, B:5.

"A Natural Rapport," *Georgetown Magazine*, Spring 2001, 18–29.

Highlands Village

Aspen, Colorado, 1996–2002

Partner: Graham S. Wyatt. Project Designers: Joseph Andriola, John Cays, Geoffrey Mouen. Assistants: Kurt Glauber, Jonas Goldberg, Haven Knight, Breen Mahony, Katherine Oudens, Dennis Sagiev, Paul Zamek, Paul Zembsch. Landscape Associate: Ann Stokes. Landscape Assistants: Mary Estes, Hannah Fusco, Gerrit Goss, Laura Hynes, Allison Towne. Associate Architects: Kendall/Heaton Associates, Cottle Graybeal Yaw Architects.

Scott Condon, "Hines Unveils His Plans for Highlands," *Aspen Times Daily*, June 16, 1993, 1, 13.

Dave Reed, "Hines Unwraps a New Highlands," *Aspen Daily News*, June 16, 1993, 1, 9.

Erin Perry, "Highlands Development a Done Deal," *Aspen Daily News*, October 30, 1997, 1, 4.

Robert A. M. Stern: Buildings and Projects, 1993–1998 (New York: The Monacelli Press, 1998), 138–39.

Nancy D. Holt, "Hines Ski Resort Project Clears the Gates," *Wall Street Journal*, January 6, 1999, B:12.

Elaine Louie, "The Cost of Living with a Ski Slope at the Back Door," *New York Times*, January 14, 1999, F:3.

"New Yorkers in the Wilderness," *Architectural Record*, February 1999, 52.

"Hines Interests: $8 Billion Gorilla Joins the Ski Village Fray," *Ski*, March–April 1999, 112.

J. Sebastian Sinisi, "Ski Villages Follow Design of Old Lodges," *Denver Post*, April 5, 1999, B:5–6, 8.

Peter Oliver, "Aspen Highlands: The Last Resort," *Aspen*, Holiday 1999–2000, 131–35, 234, 236.

"Extraordinary Properties for Sale: Aspen," *Architectural Digest*, September 2000, 199.

Brent Gardner-Smith, "All Right? All Wrong? Or Just Half-Finished?" *Aspen Times*, February 24–25, 2001, A:9–11, 21, 23.

Walter A. Rutes, Richard H. Penner, and Lawrence Adams, *Hotel Design, Planning, and Development* (New York: W. W. Norton, 2001), 102.

Federal Reserve Bank of Atlanta
Atlanta, Georgia, 1996–2001

Partner: Graham S. Wyatt. Project Architect: Michael Jones. Senior Assistants: John Ellis, Victor Jones. Assistants: Janet Antich, Kurt Glauber, Carey Jackson-Yonce, Deborah Schneiderman. Landscape Assistant: Sarah Newbery. Associate Architect: Smallwood, Reynolds, Stewart, Stewart & Associates, Inc.

Sallye Salter, "A New Face for the Fed," *Atlanta Journal & Constitution*, June 24, 1998, 1.

Catherine Fox, "Sense of Tradition Also Will Move to Midtown," *Atlanta Journal & Constitution*, June 25, 1998, G:2.

Sallye Salter, "Reserve Shows Off Plans for New Digs," *Atlanta Journal & Constitution*, June 25, 1998, G:2.

Maria Saporta, "Design Won't Strip Neighborhood Vision," *Atlanta Journal & Constitution*, June 25, 1998, G:2.

Catherine Fox, "Fed Secure in Its New Design," *Atlanta Journal & Constitution*, July 5, 1998, K:5.

Robert A. M. Stern: Buildings and Projects, 1993–1998 (New York: The Monacelli Press, 1998), 318–19.

Phil Gast, "They're Banking on It: Federal Reserve Bank's Groundwork Not Routine," *Atlanta Journal-Constitution*, May 24, 1999, E:1, 6.

Catherine Fox, "A New Beginning: Fed's Building a Behemoth in Disguise," *Atlanta Journal-Constitution*, September 10, 2001, F:6.

Heavenly View Ranch
Snowmass, Colorado, 1996–1999

Associate Partner: Randy M. Correll. Senior Assistant: Diane Boston. Assistant: Monica Chiodo. Interiors Associate: Patricia Burns Ross. Interiors Assistant: Fawn Galli.

Robert A. M. Stern: Buildings and Projects, 1993–1998 (New York: The Monacelli Press, 1998), 320–21.

Diagonal Mar Entertainment and Retail Center
Barcelona, Spain, 1996–2001

Partner: Graham S. Wyatt. Project Architects: Gary Brewer, Jonilla Dorsten. Assistants: Susan Egan, Julia Nelson, Deborah Schneiderman, Michael Wilbur. Landscape Assistant: Sarah Newbery. Associate Architect: Kendall/Heaton Associates.

Robert A. M. Stern: Buildings and Projects, 1993–1998 (New York: The Monacelli Press, 1998), 322–25.

"Diagonal Mar Named Most Innovative Real Estate Project in Barcelona," *Hinesight*, March–April 2001, 10.

El Periodico (Barcelona), November 28, 2001, 10.

Anatxu Zabalbeascoa, "Robert A. M. Stern: Toda la arquitectura es nostalgica," *El País*, December 8, 2001, 27.

"Diagonal Mar: Escape by the Sea," *Hinesight*, January–March 2002, 6–7.

Chris Nuttall, "The Convert: Developer Gerald Hines Has Learned to Love—and Profit by—the Complications of Building in Europe," *Architecture*, March 2002, 40–42.

Trisha Riggs, "Retaining Value," *Urban Land*, October 2002, 157–58.

Hobby Center for the Performing Arts
Houston, Texas, 1996–2002

Partner: Graham S. Wyatt. Associate Partner: Barry Rice. Senior Associate: Adam Anuszkiewicz. Assistants: John Cays, Hernán Chebar, Frank de Santis, Anselm Fusco, Shannon Gallagher, Dennis Giobbe, Jonas Goldberg, Edwin Hofmann, Haven Knight, John Libertino, Andreas Paul Miller, Quincey Nixon, Tamie Noponen, Dennis Sagiev, Ahmad-ali Sarder-Afkhami. Interiors Senior Associate: John Gilmer. Interiors Assistants: Peter Fleming, Fawn Galli, Claire Ratliff, Scott Sloat, Cynthia Tai, Paola Velazquez. Landscape Associate: Charlotte Frieze. Associate Architect: Morris Architects.

Clifford Pugh, "The First Look at Houston's Next Theater Center, or Stern's Grand Vision," *Houston Chronicle*, November 29, 1998, 8–10, 24.

David Dillon, "Performing Arts Hall Planned for Houston," *Dallas Morning News*, December 1, 1998, A:19, 21.

Robert A. M. Stern: Buildings and Projects, 1993–1998 (New York: The Monacelli Press, 1998), 330–33.

"Buzz," *Architecture*, January 1999, 29.

David Dillon, "The Latest in the Lone Star Lineup: Stern's Houston Arts Center," *Architectural Record*, January 1999, 47.

Nina Rappaport, "On the Drawing Boards," *Oculus*, February 1999, 4.

Mark Alden Branch, "Blast from the Past," *Yale Alumni Magazine*, March 1999, 24–31.

James Fallon, "AW2000: Architecture & Design," *W*, March 1999.

"New Contracts of the Month: Most Retro," *World Architecture*, April 1999, 24.

"Reception Honoring Robert A. M. Stern at Hobby Home," *Paper City* (Houston), April 1999.

Annette Baird, "Performing Arts Facility Breaks Ground," *Houston Chronicle*, June 9, 1999, 1, 4.

"Citelines," *Cite*, Fall–Winter 1999–2000, 4, 7.

Charles Lockwood, "Houston's Turn," *Urban Land*, February 2000, 54–59.

Ben DeSoto, "In the Art Zone," *Houston Chronicle*, May 5, 2000, A:35.

Everette Evans, "Selim Zilkha Hall Offers Intimate Seating for 500," *Houston Chronicle*, January 10, 2001, D:10.

Charles Ward, "A Lobby for the Arts," *Houston Chronicle*, January 10, 2001, D:1, 8–10.

Clifford Pugh, "Eminent Domain: Hobby Center Nears Its Gala Opening Act," *Houston Chronicle*, March 17, 2002, 10, 16.

Margaret Wazuka, "Hobby Center for the Performing Arts, Houston, Texas, by Robert A. M. Stern and Morris Architects," designarchitecture.com, April 30, 2001.

Clifford Pugh, "Producer Puts Personal Touch on Hobby Center Opening Night," *Houston Chronicle*, May 1, 2002, 1.

Clifford Pugh, "A Stellar Debut," *Houston Chronicle*, May 5, 2002, 17–18, 20.

"News in Brief: U.S.," *World Architecture*, May 2001, 27.

576   Everett Evans, "Sarofim Hall: Made for Musicals," *Houston Chronicle*, May 5, 2002, 19–20.

Clifford Pugh, "Hobby Center (Almost) a Work of Art," *Houston Chronicle*, May 10, 2002, A:1, 14.

Clifford Pugh, "Magic of Theatre: Unfinished Work Doesn't Stop Show at Hobby Debut," *Houston Chronicle*, May 11, 2002, A:1, 18.

David Dillon, "Modern Missteps in Houston," *Dallas Morning News*, May 13, 2002, 1–3.

Mitchell J. Shields, "A Sense of Invitation," *Houston Chronicle*, May 13, 2002, 1–5.

Shelby Hodge, "TUTS Celebrates a Memorable 'Evening,'" *Houston Chronicle*, May 20, 2002, 4.

Peter Brown, "Pride of Place: Architectural Icon Robert A. M. Stern Shares His Views on Houston," *Houston In-Town*, November 1, 2002, 6.

Terrence Doody, "Knowing One's Place," *Texas Architecture*, November 11, 2002, 30–33.

Malcolm Quantrill, "Where Did the Hobby Center Go Wrong?" *Cite*, Fall 2002, 26–27.

Guest House and Tennis Pavilion

Brentwood, California, 1996–1999

Associate Partner: Randy M. Correll. Senior Assistant: Naomi Neville. Landscape Associate: Charlotte Frieze. Landscape Assistant: Ashley Christopher. Interiors Associate: Patricia Burns Ross. Interiors Assistant: Fawn Galli.

Robert A. M. Stern: Buildings and Projects, 1993–1998 (New York: The Monacelli Press, 1998), 340–41.

Street Furniture for J. C. Decaux

1996–

Partner: Paul L. Whalen. Senior Assistant: Kurt Glauber. Assistant: Michael Levendusky.

Clifford J. Levy, "New Furniture—and, Finally, Toilets Planned for City Streets," *New York Times*, December 4, 1996, B:1, 7.

Wayne Barrett, "Streetscape Stall," *Village Voice*, March 31, 1998, 25.

David W. Dunlap, "Plan Seeks to Clarify Muddled Lower Manhattan," *New York Times*, July 1, 1998, B:1.

David W. Dunlap, "Street Furniture Designs Stuck in Gridlock," *New York Times*, August 9, 1998, 11:1, 16.

Herbert Muschamp, "Oh, to Be on the Boulevard with a Calling Card and You," *New York Times*, October 8, 1998, F:4.

Richard Cook, "Chairman of the Boards," *Wallpaper*, September 2001, 53–56.

Fran Spielman, "Bus Shelter Deal a Windfall for City," *Chicago Sun-Times*, July 18, 2002, 10.

"Off the Record," *Architectural Record*, August 2002, 28.

Robert C. Herguth, "Decorative Bus Shelters on Their Way," *Chicago Sun-Times*, December 9, 2002, online edition.

Broadway Residence Hall, Columbia University, and Morningside Heights Branch, New York Public Library

New York, New York, 1996–2000

BROADWAY RESIDENCE HALL Partner: Alexander P. Lamis. Associate: Christine Kelley. Assistants: Kevin Galvin, Alex Karmeinsky, Edmund Leveckis, Howard Shen, Youngmin Woo.

MORNINGSIDE HEIGHTS BRANCH Partner: Alexander P. Lamis. Project Manager: Julie Nymann. Assistants: Edmund Leveckis, Jong-Hyuck Park, Rebecca Post, Youngmin Woo, Paul Zembsch. Interiors Assistants: Sharmell Anderson, Peter Fleming, Claire Ratliff.

Hans Chen, "New Dorm Architect Proposes Plan to Area Residents," *Columbia Daily Spectator*, March 25, 1997, 1, 5.

"Postings: Fourteen-Story Residence Hall Planned for Broadway and 113th Street; A New Den for the Lions of Columbia," *New York Times*, April 20, 1997, 9:1.

"Postings: One Hundred Years on Morningside Heights; Columbia Past, Columbia Not," *New York Times*, October 26, 1997, 11:1.

David W. Dunlap, "Alma Mater Gets a Makeover," *New York Times*, November 16, 1997, 11:1, 6.

Barry Bergdoll, *Mastering McKim's Plan: Columbia's First Century on Morningside Heights* (New York: Miriam and Ira D. Wallach Art Gallery, Columbia University in the City of New York, 1997), 241–42.

David Garrard Lowe, "Urbanities: Now They're Deconstructing the Columbia Campus," *City Journal*, Autumn 1997, 84–97.

Benjamin Lowe, "$50 Million Dorm Stirs Talk," *Columbia Daily Spectator*, February 11, 1998, 1, 5.

Janet Allon, "Dormitory Plan: One Minus, Many Pluses," *New York Times*, February 22, 1998, 14:6.

Mia-Margaret Laabs, "Board Approves Proposed Dormitory," *Columbia Daily Spectator*, February 23, 1998, 1, 5.

Anne Canty, "Residence Hall Passes Hurdle with Vote of Community Board," *Columbia University Record*, February 27, 1998, 3.

Erik Seadale, "Town and Gown Marry on Columbia Dorm Plan," *New York Observer*, March 9, 1998, 10.

Kaya Tretjak, "Construction Starts on $50 Million Dorm," *Columbia Daily Spectator*, September 15, 1998, 1, 7.

Nicholas Adams, "Tschumi e Stern alla Columbia," *Casabella*, October 1998, 84–89.

Robert A. M. Stern: Buildings and Projects, 1993–1998 (New York: The Monacelli Press, 1998), 248, 250–53.

Kate Kelly, "Building Boom of 1999: Will Manhattan Change into Tacky Condo Town?" *New York Observer*, February 1, 1999, 1, 11.

Daniel Feldman, "Architect Outlines Dorm Plan," *Columbia Daily Spectator*, February 10, 1999, 1, 9.

"The Campus within the City," *Oculus*, March 1999, 3.

"Columbia Builds," *Oculus*, March 1999, 11–12.

Jordan Fox, "Technology in Residence," *American Schools and Universities*, August 1999, 111–15.

Karrie Jacobs, "Architecture 101," *New York*, October 4, 1999, 20–21.

Lauren Marshall, "New Columbia Dorm Designed by Robert A. M. Stern Opens on Broadway," www.columbia.edu, September 2000.

Alex Sachare, "Broadway Dorm Opens on Schedule," *Columbia College Today*, September 2000, 4.

Norval White and Elliot Willensky, *AIA Guide to New York City*, 4th ed. (New York: Three Rivers Press, 2000), 471.

"College Walk: A Great Place to Call Home," *Columbia*, Winter 2001, 6–7.

Shaila K. Dewan, "Nineteenth-Century Charm Saved in Twenty-First-Century Stacks," *New York Times*, June 20, 2001, B:3.

Helen Chernikoff, "University and Library Come to Terms," *West Side Spirit*, October 18, 2001, 6.

Hilary Ballon, "The Architecture of Columbia, Educational Visions in Conflict: A Battleground of Ideas, Mission, Relationship to City," *Columbia College Today*, January 2002, 14–21.

"A Sense of Place: New Facilities and Renovations Emphasize Community," *American Libraries*, April 2002, 48.

Edgewater Apartments

West Vancouver, British Columbia, Canada, 1997–2000

Associate Partner: Barry Rice. Assistants: Dennis Giobbe, Howard Shen. Landscape Associate: Charlotte Frieze. Landscape Assistant: Alessandra Galletti. Interiors Assistants: Claire Ratliff, Scott Sloat. Associate Architect: Lawrence Doyle Architect.

Susan Balcom, "Edgewater Elegance," *Vancouver Sun*, August 29, 1998, G:1, 4.

Chris Dafoe, "The Stern Approach to Building Past and Present," *Globe and Mail*, October 31, 1998, C:11.

Robert A. M. Stern: Buildings and Projects, 1993–1998 (New York: The Monacelli Press, 1998), 346–47.

Robin Ward, "15-Storey Monster House," *Vancouver Sun*, January 13, 1999, C:6.

Barbara McQuade, "The High and the Mighty," *Vancouver Sun*, November 18, 2000, C:1.

Georges Binder, *Sky High Living: Contemporary High-Rise Apartment and Mixed-Use Buildings* (Mulgrave, Australia: Images, 2002), 140–41.

Rodgers Recreation Center, Salve Regina University

Newport, Rhode Island, 1997–2000

Partner: Graham S. Wyatt. Associate Partner: Grant F. Marani. Senior Assistant: Renan Pierre. Assistants: Jamie Alexander, Jonas Goldberg, Edwin Hofmann, Tamie Noponen, Steven Petrides, Charles Toothill. Interiors Assistant: Damion Phillips. Landscape Associate: Ann Stokes. Landscape Assistants: Katherine Bennett, Dorothy Bothwell, Ashley Christopher, Hannah Fusco, Allison Towne. Associate Architect: Robinson Green Beretta.

Bob Ottaviano, "Salve Proposes New Gym," *Newport This Week*, August 28, 1997, 1, 9.

Matthias Boxler, "Rodgers Recreation Center Construction Off and Running," *Report from Newport*, Spring–Summer 1999, 26–27.

David Brussat, "The 'Campus' of Salve Regina," *Providence Journal*, January 27, 2000, B:7.

"Dedication of Rodgers Recreation Center," *Report from Newport* 27, no. 1 (2001): 24–25.

Robert A. M. Stern, "Building Fitness to an Entirely New Level," *Report from Newport* 27, no. 1 (2001): 22–23.

Paul Kenyon, "Salve's New Center as Good as . . . Old," *Providence Journal*, January 12, 2001, D:1, 4.

Mary Shepard, "Salve's Rodgers Center Reflects Region's Architectural Flavor," *Newport Daily News*, April 16, 2001, B:3.

Knott Science Center Addition, College of Notre Dame of Maryland

Baltimore, Maryland, 1997–2000

Partner: Graham S. Wyatt. Project Architect: Augusta Barone. Assistants: James Johnson, Dennis Sagiev. Landscape Associate: Ann Stokes. Associate Architect: George Vaeth Associates.

Edward Gunts, "College Making Room for Science Classes," *Baltimore Sun*, September 10, 1998, B:2.

Robert A. M. Stern: Buildings and Projects, 1993–1998 (New York: The Monacelli Press, 1998), 270–71.

Edward Gunts, "Emphasizing Science for Students," *Baltimore Sun*, April 27, 2000, B:2.

"Knott Science Center: A Facility to Awaken Wonder," *College of Notre Dame of Maryland Today*, Summer 2000, 6, 7.

"President's Gala, Celebration 2000," *College of Notre Dame of Maryland Today*, Summer 2000, 10–11.

Edward Gunts, "Ivory Towers Get More Respect," *Baltimore Sun*, September 1, 2000, 1–4.

Manzanita Hall, College of Arts, Media, and Communication, California State University, Northridge

Northridge, California, 1997–2001

Partner: Alexander P. Lamis. Associate Partner: Barry Rice. Project Architect: Anselm Fusco. Assistants: Monique Agnew, Tricia Alvez, Fred Berthelot, Frank Bostelmann, Arthur Chu, John Esposito, Matt Formicola, Zvi Gersh, Jennifer Hanlin, Stefan Mark Hare, Jae Kim, Nurçan Kisa, Mark Knoke, Nicole LaRossa, Candace Lee, Ernesto Leon, Andreas Paul Miller, Tamie Noponen, Rebecca Post, Nathan Quiring, Brock Roseberry, Heidi Sawyer, Samir Shah, Noah Shepherd, Ryan Sommers, Jonathan Toews, Aldona Tukallo, Michael Wilbur, Sandra Zenk. Landscape Associate: Dawn Handler. Landscape Assistant: Marie Andree Soundy. Interiors Assistant: Damion Phillips. Associate Architect: Fields Devereaux.

Claire Vitucci, "Cal State Northridge Razes Neutra Building," *Los Angeles Times*, July 18, 1997, B:3.

"Designs for New AMC Buildings Win College Approval," *Northridge*, Winter 1998–99, 3.

John Chandler, "Design Approved for New $16.8 Million AMC Building," www.csun.edu (California State University, Northridge), February 1, 1999, 4.

"CSUN Trustees Approve Design for Media Center," *Los Angeles Times*, February 3, 1999, B:4.

Solomon Moore, "Trustees Approve Design for $16.8 Million CSUN Complex," *Los Angeles Times*, February 3, 1999, Valley edition, B:1, 6.

"A Form to Heighten Function," *Los Angeles Times*, February 7, 1999, Valley edition, B:16.

"Buzz," *Architecture*, March 1999, 41.

Zanto Peabody, "Cal State Movie Program Steps into the Spotlight with Award," *Los Angeles Times*, May 27, 2001, B:4.

Carmen Ramos Chandler, "Manzanita Hall: New AMC Building," *Northridge*, Fall 2001, 14–17.

578 **Spangler Campus Center, Harvard Business School**

Boston, Massachusetts, 1997–2001

Partner: Graham S. Wyatt. Project Architect: Gary Brewer. Project Managers: John Berson, Kevin Smith, Susi Yu. Job Captain: Kurt Glauber. Senior Assistant: Melissa DelVecchio. Assistants: Victor Agran, Arthur Chu, Frank de Santis, Mark Gage, Jonas Goldberg, Donald Johnson, Jim Johnson, Andrei Martin, Mark Pledger, Emily Stegner, Carol Dufresne Trent, Youngmin Woo, Mohamed Yakub. Landscape Assistants: Katherine Bennett, Norbert Holter, Sung Ok. Interiors Assistants: Schuyler Blackman, Pascal Delisse, Fawn Galli, Kelly Greeson, Claire Ratliff, Scott Sloat, Joy Tucci.

"Building Business," *Harvard Magazine*, March–April 1997, 68–69.

"Student Center Deluxe," *Harvard Magazine*, September–October 1998, 76.

Judith A. Ross, "A Constructive Summer at HBS," *Harvard Business School Bulletin*, October 1999, 6.

Jim Mutugi, "Welcome to Versailles," *HARBUS* (student newspaper, Harvard Business School), January 16, 2001, 1, 4.

Robert Campbell, "Harvard's Traditional Original," *Boston Globe*, January 25, 2001, D:1, 3.

"Classics, Old & New," *Harvard Magazine*, March–April 2001, 64–65.

Douglass Shand-Tucci, *The Campus Guide: Harvard University* (New York: Princeton Architectural Press, 2001), 303–4.

James McCown, "Crossing the Great Divide," *Blueprint*, February 2002.

Robert Campbell, "Users Look for the Name Tags before Buying Architecture—or Blue Jeans—Today," *Architectural Record*, October 2002, 79.

Robert Campbell, "Urban Scrawl," *Boston Globe*, January 12, 2003, 10–13, 20–27.

The Chatham

181 East 65th Street, New York, New York, 1997–2001

Partner: Paul L. Whalen. Associate Partner: Barry Rice. Associate: Michael Jones. Assistant: Dennis Giobbe. Associate Architect: Ismael Leyva Architects.

Anthony Ramirez, "At the Sign of the Dove, a Sign of the Times," *New York Times*, February 8, 1998, C:7.

Tracie Rozhon, "Designed by Stern, but No Shingles," *New York Times*, November 22, 1998, 11:1.

Robert A. M. Stern: Buildings and Projects, 1993–1998 (New York: The Monacelli Press, 1998), 364–65.

Alan S. Oser, "How to Build with a Firm Foundation," *New York Times*, January 31, 1999, 11:1, 6.

Kate Kelly, "Building Boom of 1999: Will Manhattan Change into Tacky Condo Town?" *New York Observer*, February 1, 1999, 1, 11.

"Contracts: USA," *World Architecture*, March 1999, 31.

Susanna Sirefman, "As More Towers Sprout in New York, Major Architects Enter the Field," *Architectural Record*, March 1999, 50.

Alexandra Lange, "The Towers that Will Be," *New York*, April 12, 1999, 42–44.

Rachelle Garbarine, "Luxury Condominiums Seeing Strong Demand," *New York Times*, April 16, 1999, B:9.

"Noted Architect Designs Sales Center for Unique East 65th Street Condominium," *New York Times Magazine*, April 25, 1999, 86.

"Architects: Designers of Dreams," *New York Living*, April 1999, 38.

"Listings: Newly Opened and on the Way," *New York Living*, April 1999, 39–40, 42–43.

Della Smith, "Super Luxury Condos," *New York Living*, April 1999, 33–37.

Rachelle Garbarine, "Upper East Side Story," *New York Times*, May 30, 1999, 3:2.

"Multi Talented," *Residential Architect*, July–August 1999, 24–25.

Paul Goldberger, "The Sky Line: A Touch of Class," *New Yorker*, August 16, 1999, 86–88, 90.

Norval White and Elliot Willensky, *AIA Guide to New York*, 4th ed. (New York: Three Rivers Press, 2000), 439.

Braden Keil, "Park View Penthouse," *Gotham*, March 2001, 260.

Tracie Rozhon, "Condos on the Rise, by Architectural Stars," *New York Times*, July 19, 2001, F:1, 10.

Maura McEvoy, "Fifteen Rooms, River View," *Town & Country*, July 2001, 102–7, 116, 125, 130.

Victor Wishna, "Visions of Grandeur," *Avenue*, April 2002, 30–38.

Stephen M. L. Aronson, "Robert A. M. Stern: The Architect's Creation Stands Tall in Manhattan," *Architectural Digest*, September 2002, 197–203, 289.

Georges Binder, *Sky High Living: Contemporary High-Rise Apartment and Mixed-Use Buildings* (Mulgrave, Australia: Images, 2002), 156–57, 241.

Apartment in the Chatham

New York, New York, 1998–2001

Partner: Roger H. Seifter. Project Manager: Victoria Baran. Project Architect: Deborah Wilen-Cohen. Assistant: Dennis Giobbe. Interiors Senior Associate: John Gilmer. Interiors Assistants: Fawn Galli, Kelly Greeson, Joy Tucci.

Stephen M. L. Aronson, "Robert A. M. Stern: The Architect's Creation Stands Tall in Manhattan," *Architectural Digest*, September 2002, 197–203, 289.

Frank and Susan Bescher, letter to the editor, *Architectural Digest*, October 2002, 35.

The Seville

300 East 77th Street, New York, New York, 1997–2002

Partner: Alexander P. Lamis. Associate Partner: Barry Rice. Associates: Hernán Chebar, Michael Jones. Assistant: Steven Petrides. Interiors Senior Associate: John Gilmer. Interiors Associate: Scott Sloat. Interiors Assistants: Cynthia Smith, Georgette Sturam. Associate Architect: SLCE Architects.

Alan S. Oser, "A Rental Builder Shifts to High Gear," *New York Times*, June 21, 1998, 11:1, 6.

Robert A. M. Stern: Buildings and Projects, 1993–1998 (New York: The Monacelli Press, 1998), 368–69.

Kate Kelly, "Building Boom of 1999: Will Manhattan Change into Tacky Condo Town?" *New York Observer*, February 1, 1999, 1, 11.

Alexandra Lange, "The Towers that Will Be," *New York*, April 12, 1999, 42–44.

F. Peter Model, "They'll Take Manhattan: RFR/Davis," *New York Living*, December 1999, 22–27.

Rachelle Garbarine, "A Partnership Is Thriving on Luxury Apartment Projects," *New York Times*, April 28, 2000, B:8.

"RFR/Davis: A Hi-End Niche Player," *New York Living*, May 2001, 56–57.

David S. Chartock, "High-Strength Concrete Provides Layout Flexibility for the Seville," *New York Construction News*, July 2001, 45–49.

Jonathan Mahler, "Gotham Rising," *Talk*, December 2001–January 2002, 120–25, 148–52.

James Gardner, "A Promising Combination," *New York Sun*, May 20, 2002, 10.

Aging and Allied Health Building and Gill Heart Institute, University of Kentucky Medical Center

Lexington, Kentucky, 1998–2003

Partners: Grant F. Marani, Graham S. Wyatt. Associate: Douglas Wright. Assistant: Frank de Santis. Associate Architects: CMW (Chrisman Miller Woodford), FKP (The Falick/Klein Partnership).

Dream House for *This Old House* Magazine

Wilton, Connecticut, 1998–1999

Senior Associate, Design: Gary Brewer. Senior Associate, Construction: Daniel Lobitz. Project Manager: Deborah Wilen-Cohen. Assistants: Shannon Gallagher, Haven Knight, Tamie Noponen, Miriam Torres-Marcos.

Jenny Allen, "Dream House," *This Old House*, July–August 1998, 74–81.

Curtis Rist, "Born in America," *This Old House*, September–October 1998, 71–76.

Beth Longware Duff, "This 'New' House," *Wilton Villager*, October 1, 1998, B:1.

Jack McClintock, "Upon This Rock," *This Old House*, November 1998, 122–23.

Curtis Rist, "Designing a Proper Entrance," *This Old House*, December 1998, 61, 64.

"Steal These Looks," *This Old House*, December 1998, 98–103.

Robert A. M. Stern: Buildings and Projects, 1993–1998 (New York: The Monacelli Press, 1998), 380–81.

Brad Lemley, "Good Bones," *This Old House*, January–February 1999, 88–93.

Curtis Rist, "Cabin Fever," *This Old House*, January–February 1999, 53–54.

Jack McClintock, "Stone Faced," *This Old House*, March 1999, 102–8.

Rob Schweitzer, "This New House," *Wilton Bulletin*, June 17, 1999, A:1, 20.

Jack McClintock, "Great Panes," *This Old House*, June 1999, 94–96.

Beth Longware Duff, "Local Designer Creates 'This Old House' Interiors," *Wilton Villager*, July 29, 1999, A:3.

Brad Lemley, "Hot Stuff Way Cool," *This Old House*, July–August 1999, 108–12.

Curtis Rist, "Shades of Summer," *This Old House*, July–August 1999, 63, 65.

Curtis Rist, "Site Seeing," *This Old House*, July–August 1999, 113.

Brad Lemley, "Fitting Trim," *This Old House*, September 1999, 112–16, 118.

Beth Longware Duff, "This Old House Opens Its Doors to Public," *Wilton Villager*, October 7, 1999, A:6.

Beth Longware Duff, "Wilton 'Dream House' a Hit with Public," *Wilton Villager*, October 14, 1999, B:3.

Curtis Rist, "Wall Smarts," *This Old House*, October 1999, 110–15.

Curtis Rist, "Dream House: Bathed in Luxury," *This Old House*, November 1999, 114–18.

Curtis Rist, "A Dream Come True," *This Old House*, December 1999, 101–16.

Donna Sapolin, "Letter From *This Old House*: Dream Housewarming," *This Old House*, December 1999, 85.

"At the Hub," *This Old House Kitchen and Bath*, Winter 2001, 58.

Curtis Rist, "Lot of Light, Space, and Top-Quality Materials Turn This Master Bath into a Private Sanctuary," *This Old House Kitchen and Bath*, Winter 2001, 84–86, 88.

Miami Beach Library and Collins Park Cultural Center

Miami Beach, Florida, 1998–2003

Partner: Alexander P. Lamis. Associate: Christine Kelley. Project Managers: Salvador Peña-Figueroa, Rebecca Post. Senior Assistants: Tamie Noponen, Michael Wilbur. Assistants: Arthur Chu, John Esposito, Michael Flaherty, Anselm Fusco, Jeff Hendricks, Charles Toothill. Interiors Senior Assistant: Damion Phillips. Interiors Assistants: Peter Fleming, Scott Sloat, Joy Tucci. Landscape Associates: Dawn Handler, Marsh Kriplen. Landscape Senior Assistants: Gerrit Goss, Norbert Holter. Landscape Assistants: Valerie Alexander, Katherine Bennett, Laurie Hynes, Ann Stokes. Associate Architect: Borrelli & Associates.

Peter Whoriskey, "Top Firms Vying for the Honor," *Miami Herald*, May 25, 1998, B:1–2.

Richard M. Buck, "Collins Park Cultural Campus Moves Forward," *Miami Design Preservation League Impressions*, Summer 1998, 1, 3–4.

Herbert Muschamp, "Designs for Students, Stars and Travelers," *New York Times*, September 13, 1998, 2:119–21.

Beth Dunlop, "Correspondent's File: Pastels and Preservationists: Miami Beach Navigates the Tension between Heritage and Contemporary Design," *Architectural Record*, August 1999, 45, 47, 49.

"Robert A. M. Stern Architects with Borelli & Associates, Regional Library," *Abitare*, May 24, 2000, 157.

Mike Seemuth, "Lost Horizon," *Ocean Drive*, June 15, 2000, 185–89.

Herbert Muschamp, "Contemplative Interiors, Private Gardens and a Trump Tower," *New York Times*, September 10, 2000, 2:100.

Raul A. Barreneche, "For a Library, Robert Stern Shows His Take on Modernism," *New York Times*, January 18, 2001, F:3.

"Metro: Miami Beach," *Metropolitan Home*, July–August 2001, 48.

Neisen Kasdin, "Miami Beach: Urban Tropical Deco," *Urban Land*, October 2002, 81.

Torre del Ángel

Reforma 350, Mexico City, Mexico, 1998–2000

Partner: Graham S. Wyatt. Associate: Meghan McDermott. Assistants: Ryan Hullinger, Alex Karmeinsky, Ernesto Leon, John Mueller, Renan Pierre. Associate Architect: Kendall/Heaton Associates.

"Class A Office Building," *Wall Street Journal*, December 2, 1998, B:12.

"Corrections and Amplifications," *Wall Street Journal*, December 3, 1998, A:2.

Robert A. M. Stern: Buildings and Projects, 1993–1998 (New York: The Monacelli Press, 1998), 382–83.

Carolyn O'Shields, "Torre del Ángel Design Unveiled," *Hinesight*, March–April 1999, 2.

Alejandra Sanchez, "Nace un nuevo edificio," *Suplemento Entre Nuevos Periodico Reforma*, May 1999.

Juan B. Dolores G., "Llega un nuevo Ángel a Mexico," *Arquitectura y Diseño Internacional*, 1999, 18.

"A la cabeza de un gran equipo," *Arquitectura y Diseño Internacional*, 2000, 40–43.

"Ante el reto de un contexto," *Arquitectura y Diseño Internacional*, 2000, 48–51.

Daniel Chavez, "Inauguracion del edificio Torre del Ángel: Un nuevo logro Hines," *Arquitectura y Diseño Internacional*, 2000, 16.

Roxana Fabris, "Concretando ideas,"*Arquitectura y Diseño Internacional*, 2000, 60–63.

Roxana Fabris, "Mas que un reflejo," *Arquitectura y Diseño Internacional*, 2000, 52–59.

"Visualizando el exito," *Arquitectura y Diseño Internacional*, 2000, 44–47.

"Torre del Ángel: A Landmark Building in Mexico City," *Hinesight*, March–April 2001, 6–7.

Nashville Public Library

Nashville, Tennessee, 1998–2001

Partner: Alexander P. Lamis. Project Designers/Managers: Jeffery Povero, Paul Zembsch. Assistants: Melissa DelVecchio, Mark Gage, Ernesto Leon, Daniel Lobitz, Andrei Martin, Julie Nymann, Jong-Hyuck Park, Salvador Peña-Figueroa, Jonathan Toews, Charles Toothill, Susi Yu. Landscape Senior Assistant: Mei Wu. Landscape Assistants: Gerrit Goss, Dawn Handler, John Merrit, Marie Andree Soundy. Interiors Senior Assistants: Thu Do, Kelly Greeson. Interiors Assistants: Claire Ratliff, Patricia Burns Ross. Associate Architect: Hart Freeland Roberts.

Rob Moritz, "Library Finds New Home on Church Street," *Nashville Paper*, March 13, 1998, A:1, 2.

Christine Kreyling, "Booking Space: Who'll Design the New Library?" *Nashville Scene*, April 9, 1998, 16–21, 23–24.

Rob Moritz, "Library Designs Down to Three," *Tennessean*, June 23, 1998, 1–2.

Elizabeth S. Betts, "Some Architects Rate Top Design as Timeless, Others as Timeworn," *Tennessean*, June 25, 1998, 2.

Bonna M. de la Cruz, "Library Steals Page from Classics," *Tennessean*, June 25, 1998, 1.

Christine Kreyling, "In Limited Edition: The Library Designs Were Intriguing—but Who Saw Them?" *Nashville Scene*, June 25, 1998, 18–21.

Christine Kreyling, "City Limits: Reading between the Lines," *Nashville Scene*, July 2, 1998, 13–14.

Jack B. Hastings, "Architectural Digest," *Nashville Scene*, August 13, 1998.

Soren Larson, "Stern's New Nashville Library Is a Nod to Local Classicism," *Architectural Record*, August 1998, 44.

Michael J. O'Connor, "Classic Stern," *Architecture*, August 1998, 25.

Rob Moritz, "Library Designer Hits Snag," *Tennessean*, November 11, 1998, B:5.

Christine Kreyling, "Style Takes a Back Seat to Organization," *Competitions*, Fall 1998, 9–13.

Robert A. M. Stern: Buildings and Projects, 1993–1998 (New York: The Monacelli Press, 1998), 384–89.

"Public Library of Nashville and Davidson County under Construction, Completion 2000," *Rotations*, June 14, 1999, 1.

Elizabeth S. Betts, "Nashville Getting a Feel for New Library Furnishings," *Tennessean*, September 11, 1999, D:1.

Beverly Goldberg, "Library Signage," *American Libraries*, September 1999, 16.

Camille Moffitt, "Downtown Library Is Running on Schedule and under Budget," *Nashville Record*, January 13, 2000, 1, 3.

Elizabeth S. Betts, "Books & Mortar . . . with a Touch of Green," *Tennessean*, May 7, 2000, D:1, 3.

Rodney Wilson, "New Main Library Will Be Worth Checking Out," *A Level Line* (newsletter, Nashville Branch of the American Society of Civil Engineers), June 2000, 1, 4.

"Nashville Gathers $4.5 Million towards New Main Library," *Library Hotline*, July 24, 2000, 1.

R. W. Apple Jr., "Polishing Nashville's Twang," *New York Times*, July 28, 2000, E:27, 36.

"$1.65 Million Grant to Nashville Enhances Facilities, Books," *Library Hotline*, September 25, 2000, 2.

Bill Carey, "With New Library Eight Months Away, Staff Hoping Banner Archives Meet Expectations," *Nashville Post* 1, no. 11 (2000): 4–5.

Anne Paine, "Art, Books and Music Take the Spotlight Downtown," *Tennessean*, March 11, 2001, 1, A:7.

Anita Wadhwani, "Unfinished New Library Impresses First Tours," *Tennessean*, April 1, 2001, 2.

Anne Paine, "Reading Room Is Focal Point of New Downtown Library," *Tennessean*, April 30, 2001, online edition.

Anne Paine, "Metro's New Library No Mere Book Repository," *Tennessean*, May 7, 2001, online edition.

Alan Bostick, "New Library Gets Finishing Touches," *Tennessean*, June 5, 2001, A:1.

Wanda Southerland, "Grand Opening for a Grand Downtown Library," *Nashville Today*, June 7, 2001, A:1, 11.

Elizabeth Betts, "Classic Look, Modern Touch," *Tennessean*, June 8, 2001, D:1, 3.

Anne Paine, "New Library Impresses Party Guests," *Tennessean*, June 8, 2001, B:1.

"Great Library, Great City," *Tennessean*, June 9, 2001, A:14.

Anne Paine, "Library Offers New 'Promise' for Greatness," *Tennessean*, June 9, 2001, A:1.

Anne Paine and Christian Bottorff, "Library Debut a Real Page-Turner," *Tennessean*, June 10, 2001, A:1, 17.

Michael Owen, "Music City Masterpiece: Nashville Unveils $52 Million Central Library," *Columbus Ledger-Enquirer*, July 8, 2001, F:1, 4.

Michael Owen, "Nashville Does It Right," *Columbus Ledger-Enquirer*, July 8, 2001, F:2.

P. Douglas Filaroski, "Nashville's Novel Idea a Preview for Jacksonville," *Florida Times-Union*, July 20, 2001, A:1, 13.

"If It Weren't For Margaret Ann Robinson, Nashville Wouldn't Have a New Downtown Library," *Nashville Scene*, December 27, 2001, 17–22.

Bette-Lee Fox, "Keep on Constructin'," *Library Journal*, December 2001, 48, 54–55.

"From the Offices: Public Library of Nashville and Davidson County, Nashville, Tennessee," *Classicist* 6 (2001): 44–45.

Christine Kreyling, "Nashville Public Library," *Architectural Record*, February 2003, 158–61.

James Howard Kunsler, "Nashville: Skyline Revisited," *Metropolis*, February 2003, 92–96, 116–19.

Clifford A. Pearson, "Hubs of Learning," *Architectural Record*, February 2003, 151.

Peter Jay Sharp Boathouse
Swindler Cove Park, Upper Manhattan, New York, New York, 1998–

Associate Partner: Armand LeGardeur. Assistant: Audrey Rae.

Jonathan Mandell, "Always Divine, Now Garbage Has Made Her a Saint," *New York Times*, November 17, 1999, H:10.

"Art Commission Awards: Eight Honored for Excellence in Design," *New York Times*, February 27, 2000, 11:1.

Kira L. Gould, "Art Commission Honors Outstanding City Projects," *Oculus*, April 2000, 17.

"Design that Makes a Difference," *Metropolitan Home*, March–April 2001, 86.

"The Peter Jay Sharp Foundation Endows NYRP Boathouse at Swindler Cove," *Good Dirt* (newsletter, New York Restoration Project), Fall 2002.

Clearwater Public Library
Clearwater, Florida, 2001–2003

Partner: Alexander P. Lamis. Project Manager/Designer: Salvador Peña-Figueroa. Senior Assistant: Paul Zembsch. Assistant: Julie Nymann. Interiors Senior Associate: John Gilmer. Interiors Assistant: Sharmell Anderson. Landscape Associate: Marsh Kriplen. Associate Architect: Harvard Jolly Clees Toppe.

G. G. Rigsby, "Building a Better Image," *St. Petersburg Times*, January 17, 1999, online edition.

G. G. Rigsby, "Built to Last . . . or Built Too Fast?" *Clearwater Times*, January 17, 1999, 1, 11.

G. G. Rigsby, "Clearwater, Architect Urges Yes Vote on Redevelopment Plan," *Business Journal*, July 5, 2000, online edition.

Lesley Collins, "Clearwater Unveils Plans for Library," *Tampa Tribune*, May 5, 2001, Florida Metro edition, 5.

Christina Headrick, "Library's Design Looks to Past, Future," *Clearwater Times*, May 6, 2001, 1, 10.

Lesley Collins, "Eckerds Vow to Match $2 Million for Library," *Tampa Tribune*, May 10, 2001, online edition.

Leon M. Tucker, "Eckerds Gift Boosts Library Fund Drive," *St. Petersburg Times*, May 10, 2001, online edition.

Diane Steinle, "Library Puts Commissioners in Uncomfortable Role," *St. Petersburg Times*, July 22, 2001, online edition.

Christina Headrick, "At Library, Upstairs Gets 218 Feet Closer," *St. Petersburg Times*, August 15, 2001, online edition.

Christina Headrick, "Tall Condos and Design for Library Win Favor," *Clearwater Times*, September 21, 2001, 1, 3.

Jane Meinhardt, "New Library Improves View in Downtown Clearwater," *Business Journal*, November 8–14, 2002, 27.

"Graceful Shape of New Library Defies Critics," *St. Petersburg Times*, December 26, 2002, online edition.

Perkins Visitor Center, Wave Hill
Riverdale, The Bronx, New York, 1998–2003

Partner: Alexander P. Lamis. Senior Associate: Gary Brewer. Project Managers: Edmund Leveckis, Julie Nymann, James Park, Lenore Passavanti, Salvador Peña-Figueroa. Assistants: Abdessamia Aamraoui, Elena Bresciani, Julia Katrin Buse, Cedric Carle, Alex de Looz, Lindsey Douglas, Anthony Goldsby, Stefan Hare, Laura Hinton, Harry Kim, Nicole LaRossa, Halle Markus, Ernesto Martinez, Hollace Metzger, Julie Nymann, Nicolas Oudin, Christopher Podstawski, Rebecca Post, Thorsten Reinhardt, Brock Roseberry, Samir Shah, Noah Shepherd, Aldona Tukallo, Derek Willis. Landscape Associates: Dawn Handler, Marsh Kriplen. Landscape Assistants: Christina Belton, Katherine Bennett, Sung Ok. Interiors Assistants: Miriam Gelo, Ken Stuckenschneider, Georgette Sturam.

"A Decade of Change," *Riverdale Press*, June 15, 2000, A:14.

"The Future," *Wave Hill 2000 Annual Report*, 17.

"The Sources of Support," *Wave Hill 2000 Annual Report*, 13.

"For Wave Hill, a $4 Million Visitor Center," *New York Times*, June 3, 2001, 11:1.

"Perkins Visitor Center at Wave Hill," *Metropolitan Historic Structures Association*, Autumn 2001, 1.

"Perkins Visitor Center Update," *Wave Hill News*, Spring 2002, 5.

Product Design
2001–2002

SASAKI Partner: Paul L. Whalen. Senior Associate: John Gilmer. Associate: Nancy Thiel. Assistants: Qu Kim, Richard Wachter.

HBF TEXTILES Partner: Paul L. Whalen. Senior Associate: John Gilmer.

Robert A. M. Stern: Buildings and Projects, 1993–1998 (New York: The Monacelli Press, 1998), 204–5.

Randi Danforth, "Nature Calls," *Robb Report Collection*, January 2002, 35.

582 **Classroom Academic Building and Communications Technology Complex, Indiana University/Purdue University**
Indianapolis, Indiana, 1998–2003

Partner: Graham S. Wyatt. Associate: Kevin Smith. Senior Assistant: Dennis Sagiev. Assistants: Marina Berendeeva, Meredith Colon, Jeremy Edmunds, Anselm Fusco, Ole Sondresen. Associate Architect: Ratio Architects.

Greg Jefferson, "IUPUI Lands in Center of Internet2 Limelight," *Indianapolis Business Journal*, September 14–20, 1998, 26–27.

A. J. Schneider, "IUPUI Tech Building to Serve as Gateway: Center Designers Face Wiring Challenges," *Indianapolis Business Journal*, June 4, 2000, 19.

Dean's Loft
New Haven, Connecticut, 1998–1999

Partner: Roger H. Seifter. Project Manager: Victoria Baran. Interiors Senior Assistant: Fawn Galli.

Julie V. Iovine, "A Dean's Remodeling Job: Himself," *New York Times*, July 1, 1999, F:1, 6.

"The Katz Meow," *Harper's Bazaar*, April 2000, 152.

"At Home with . . . Robert A. M. Stern," *Homestyle*, March 2001, 124.

Residence
Tidewater, Virginia, 1999–

Partner: Roger H. Seifter. Project Manager: Tom Hickey. Assistants: Thomas Garland, Henry Gunawan. Landscape Architect: Ann Stokes.

Campus Community Center, Mission Bay Campus, University of California, San Francisco
San Francisco, California, Competition, 1999

Partner: Graham S. Wyatt. Senior Associate: Adam Anuszkiewicz.

Bryant Landing Senior Residence
Roslyn, New York, 1999–

Partner: Paul L. Whalen. Associate: Kevin O'Connor. Assistant: Qu Kim. Associate Architect: SLCE Architects.

Joe Scotchie, "Public Hearing on Housing Plan," *Roslyn News*, June 24, 1999, 1, 7.

Zubiarte Retail and Leisure Center
Bilbao, Spain, 1999–

Partner: Paul L. Whalen. Senior Associate: Adam Anuszkiewicz. Project Architect: Sargent Gardiner. Project Manager: Nancy Thiel. Senior Assistants: Jason Hwang, Michael McClure, Mike Soriano, Miriam Torres-Marcos. Assistants: Veronica Caminos, Johnny Cruz, Gregory Horgan, Yusung Hwang, Andrei Martin, Corina Rugeroni, Jeff Straesser, Richard Wachter, Lindsay Weiss. Associate Architects: IDOM, LKS Ingenieria.

Whitney Gould, "From Spain, a Model of Rebuilding with Vision," *Milwaukee Journal Sentinel*, April 23, 2000, online edition.

José Mari Reviriego, "Abandoibarra abrira su centro comercial en 2003 y primara el ocio y la moda," *El Correo*, February 20, 2001, 2–3.

"Abandoibarra presenta su 'corazón' comercial,"*El Correo*, May 3, 2001, 1.

Xabier Ga Arguello, "El centro comercial de Abandoibarra sera inaugurado la primavera del año 2003," *Bizkaia*, May 3, 2001, 24.

José Mari Reviriego, "Nuestra parcela es mejor que la del Guggenheim," *El Correo*, May 3, 2001, 3.

Olga Saez, "Zubiarte sera un complejo de calles con 60 comercios," *DEIA*, May 3, 2001, 3.

María José Tomé, "Abandoibarra estrenara el mayor centro de ocio y compras de Bilbao con 60 comercios," *El Correo*, May 3, 2001, 2.

John L. Vogelstein '52 Dormitory, Taft School
Watertown, Connecticut, 1999–2002

Partner: Graham S. Wyatt. Project Designer: Jeffery Povero. Project Manager: Malaika Kim. Senior Assistants: John Cays, Edmund Leveckis. Assistants: Gordon Cousins, Elise Geiger, Donald Johnson, Scott Kruger, Jonathan Toews. Interiors Senior Associate: John Gilmer. Interiors Assistants: Vennie Lau, Ken Stuckenschneider, Joy Tucci. Landscape Assistants: Norbert Holter, Sung Ok.

"Gift by Nancy and Holcombe Green Supports New Dormitory," *Campaign News* (The Campaign for Taft), September 1999, 5.

Linda Beyus, "The Dedication," *Taft Bulletin*, Fall 2002, 14–21.

Bill Miller, "The John L. Vogelstein Dormitory," *Taft Bulletin*, Fall 2002, 14–21.

626 West Main
Louisville, Kentucky, 1999–2002

Partner: Graham S. Wyatt. Senior Associate: Meghan McDermott. Assistants: John Ellis, Julie Nymann, Yuri Zagorin. Associate Architect: K. Norman Berry Associates.

John R. Karmann III, "Brown-Forman's Main Street Site to House Offices, Retail," *Business First* (Louisville), November 19, 1999.

Sheldon S. Shafer, "Old Bernheim Due Renovation," *Courier-Journal* (Louisville), November 19, 1999.

Residence in Bel Air
Los Angeles, California, 1999–2003

Partner: Randy M. Correll. Project Manager: Veronica Caminos. Senior Assistant: Youngmin Woo. Assistants: Cristiana Gallo, Yusung Hwang, Nicolas Oudin. Landscape Senior Assistant: Ashley Christopher. Landscape Assistant: Michael Weber.

A. James Clark Hall, Whitaker Biomedical Engineering Institute, Johns Hopkins University
Baltimore, Maryland, 1999–2001

Partner: Graham S. Wyatt. Senior Associate: Augusta Barone. Senior Assistants: Jeffery Povero, Dennis Sagiev. Assistants: Meredith Colon, Zvi Gersh, Christina Spaulding, Paul Zembsch. Associate Architect: HLM Design.

Phil Sneiderman, "Clark Hall Construction to Begin," *JHU Gazette* (Johns Hopkins University), October 4, 1999, 1, 4.

Edward Gunts, "Ivory Towers Get More Respect," *Baltimore Sun*, September 1, 2000, 1–4.

Edward Gunts, "From the Sensuous to the Studious," *Baltimore Sun*, November 4, 2001.

Residence at West Tisbury
Martha's Vineyard, Massachusetts, 1999–2003

Partner: Randy M. Correll. Associate: Catherine Popple. Assistants: Josh Bull, Thomas Morbitzer, Lisa Shire. Landscape Associate: Dawn Handler. Landscape Assistant: Gerrit Goss.

Arnhem City Center
Arnhem, The Netherlands, 1999–

Partner: Paul L. Whalen. Senior Associate: Daniel Lobitz. Senior Assistant: Joel Mendelson. Assistant: Chuck Toothill. Associate Architects: Beekink + Molenaar, Inbo Architects.

Bearings
Seal Harbor, Maine, 1999–2002

Associate Partner: Armand LeGardeur. Senior Assistant: Mark Pledger.

Jesse H. Jones Graduate School of Business Management, Rice University
Houston, Texas, 1999–2002

Partner: Graham S. Wyatt. Senior Associate: Adam Anuszkiewicz. Senior Assistants: John Ellis, Malaika Kim, James Park, Jeffery Povero, Sean Tobin. Assistants: Jeremy Edmunds, Andrei Martin, Miriam Torres-Marcos. Interiors Assistants: Sharmell Anderson, Kelly Greeson. Associate Architect: Morris Architects.

Ned Cramer, "On the Boards," *Architecture*, May 2001, 74–75.

Stephen Fox, *The Campus Guide: Rice University* (New York: Princeton Architectural Press, 2001), 21, 108, 126.

The Westminster
180 West 20th Street, New York, New York, 1999–2002

Partner: Paul L. Whalen. Associate Partner: Barry Rice. Associate Project Architect: Michael Jones. Associate Project Manager: Hernán Chebar. Assistants: Qu Kim, Steven Petrides, Richard Wachter, Mohamed Yakub. Interiors Senior Associate: John Gilmer. Interiors Senior Assistants: Virginia Cornell, Ken Stuckenschneider. Associate Architect: Ismael Leyva Architects.

Lore Croghan, "Related Enters Chelsea after Zoning Change," *Crain's New York Business*, December 11–17, 2000, 38.

"Special Report: Commercial Real Estate," *Crain's New York Business*, January 15, 2001, 38.

"NYL Rental Building Guide," *New York Living*, May 2001, 121.

Jonathan Mahler, "Gotham Rising," *Talk*, December 2001–January 2002, 120–25, 148–52.

Rachelle Garbarine, "Three Rental Buildings Reflect Shift in Flower District," *New York Times*, March 29, 2002, B:6.

479 Thornall Avenue
Edison Township, New Jersey, 1999–

Partner: Graham S. Wyatt. Senior Assistants: Gregory Christopher, Edwin Hofmann. Assistants: Jennifer Berlly, Aristotelis Dimitrakopoulos, Antonio Ng, Dennis Sagiev, Thomas Salazar.

Residence in Edgartown
Martha's Vineyard, Massachusetts, 1999–2003

Partner: Randy M. Correll. Project Manager: Daniel Teske. Assistants: Michael Flaherty, Yusung Hwang, Martin Russocki. Landscape Assistant: Mei Wu.

Residence
Salt Spring Island, British Columbia, Canada, 1999–

Partner: Grant F. Marani. Associate: Douglas Wright. Project Manager: Lenore Passavanti. Assistants: Marcus Carter, Elise Geiger, Eric Hofmann, Jason Hwang, Jong-Hyuck Park, Kimberly Raspanti, Charles Toothill, Daniel Wolfskehl. Interiors Senior Associate: John Gilmer. Interiors Senior Assistant: Kelly Greeson. Interiors Assistants: Amie Haugh, Joy Tucci.

K. C. Irving Environmental Science Centre and Harriet Irving Botanical Gardens, Acadia University
Wolfville, Nova Scotia, Canada, 1998–2002

Partner: Graham S. Wyatt. Senior Associate: Preston Gumberich. Associate: Geoffrey Mouen. Senior Assistant: Alex Karmeinsky. Assistants: Fred Berthelot, John Cays, Elise Geiger, Jonas Goldberg, Breen Mahony, Antonio Ng, George Punnoose. Interiors Assistants: Virginia Cornell, Amie Haugh, Vennie Lau, Scott Sloat. Associate Architect: Connor Architects & Planners. Associate Landscape Architect: Novell Tullett Landscape Architects.

Gordon Delaney, "Acadia to Build Botanical Centre," *Halifax Chronicle Herald*, March 26, 1999, 24.

Gordon Delaney, "Acadia Science Centre to Be Top-Flight Facility," *Halifax Chronicle Herald*, March 27, 1999, A:4.

"Stand Up and Cheer at Acadia," *Halifax Chronicle Herald*, March 30, 1999, B:1.

Peter McLaughlin, "YNN's Upside Dismissed Too Quickly, Teacher Says," *Halifax Daily News*, April 5, 1999, 6.

"Robert A. M. Stern Architects to Design Environmental Sciences Research Centre, Botanical Gardens, and Campus Meeting Place," www.acadiau.ca/news/stern.com (Nova Scotia, Canada: Office of Public Affairs, Acadia University, 1999).

Andrea Heans, "Irving Centre to Open in Spring, Summer," *Athenaeum* 64 (January 22, 2002): 1.

"The Gift: The K. C. Irving Environmental Science Centre and Harriet Irving Botanical Gardens," *East by Northeast*, Winter 2002–2003, 2, 6–7, 18–31.

Campus Plan, Acadia University
Wolfville, Nova Scotia, Canada, 1999–2000

Partner: Graham S. Wyatt. Senior Assistant: Jeffery Povero. Assistants: Donald Johnson, Jonathan Toews.

Residence Advantage Plan, Acadia University
Wolfville, Nova Scotia, 1999–

MASTER PLAN Partner: Graham S. Wyatt. Project Designer: Jeffery Povero. Project Manager: Donald Johnson.

EATON HOUSE Partner: Graham S. Wyatt. Project Designer: Jeffery Povero. Project Manager: Donald Johnson. Assistant: Dana Gulling. Interiors Assistant: Vennie Lau.

584 WHITMAN HOUSE Partner: Graham S. Wyatt. Project Designer: Jeffery Povero. Project Manager: Donald Johnson. Assistant: John Cays. Interiors Assistant: Vennie Lau.

NEW RESIDENCE HALLS A AND B Partner: Graham S. Wyatt. Project Designer: Jeffery Povero. Project Manager: Donald Johnson. Assistants: John Cays, Kurt Glauber. Interiors Assistants: Vennie Lau, Marie-Faye Ngo, Ken Stuckenschneider.

Residence Hall, Brooklyn Law School
Brooklyn, New York, 2000–2003

Partner: Paul L. Whalen. Associate: Hernán Chebar. Project Manager: Kevin O'Connor. Assistants: Jason Hwang, Julie Nymann, Corina Rugeroni, Oscar Sanchez, Susi Yu. Associate Architect: SLCE Architects.

Tara Bahrampour, "A Native Son to Design for the Law School," *New York Times*, May 27, 2001, 14:7.

Lore Croghan, "Downtown Brooklyn Dead Zone Shows Signs of New Life," *Crain's New York Business*, June 4–10, 2001, 19–20.

Greg Wilson, "Brooklyn Law School Eyes New Dorm to Ease Crunch," *New York Daily News*, April 14, 2002, 4.

Tara Bahrampour, "Quaker, Unlikely Actors in a Building Squabble," *New York Times*, May 5, 2002, 14:8.

Errol Louis, "Downtown Brooklyn Prefers a Jail to a Law Dorm," *New York Sun*, May 29, 2002, 6.

Errol Louis, "Plan for Law School Dorm Draws Heavy Fire: Variance to Double Height Is Called 'Spot Zoning Disguise,'" *New York Sun*, May 30, 2002, 3.

David W. Dunlap, "In Downtown Brooklyn, Too Tall Suddenly Fits," *New York Times*, July 4, 2002, B:3.

Nathaniel R. Jones Federal Building and United States Courthouse
Youngstown, Ohio, 2000–2002

Partner: Grant F. Marani. Project Manager: Paul Zembsch. Senior Assistant: Rebecca Post. Assistant: Marcus Carter. Interiors Senior Associate: John Gilmer. Interiors Assistant: Sharmell Anderson. Landscape Associate: Marsh Kriplen. Associate Architect: URS Greiner Woodward Clyde.

Sara Moss, "Coming to a City near You," *Architecture*, January 2001, 128–30.

Federal Building United States Courthouse, Youngstown, Ohio (Washington, D.C.: General Services Administration, 2002).

Vision + Voice: Design Excellence in Federal Architecture: Building Legacy (Washington, D.C.: General Services Administration, 2002), 50–52.

John C. Kuehner, "An Environmental Investment for the Future," *Plain Dealer*, March 23, 2003, 226–36.

Pennsylvania Plaza
Philadelphia, Pennsylvania, 2000–

Partner: Graham S. Wyatt. Senior Associate: Meghan McDermott. Associate: Kevin O'Connor. Senior Assistants: Don Lee, Jack Robbins. Assistants: Giovanna Albretti, Goil Amornvivat, Daniel Arbelaez, Phillipe Bihet, Steven Chua, Dariel Cobb, Aristotelis Dimitrakopoulos, Jeremy Edmunds, Edwin Hofmann, Leonid Khanin, Seung Jun Lee, Thomas Manley, Jennifer Newsom, Mike Soriano, Jeff Straesser, Robie Wood. Associate Architect: Kendall/Heaton Associates, Inc.

"High Rise Rouse," *Philadelphia Inquirer*, December 21, 2000.

Henry J. Holcomb, "Stern Will Design New Skyscraper," *Philadelphia Inquirer*, February 18, 2001, C:1, 9.

Henry J. Holcomb, "Developers Court Comcast for a Project of Magnitude," *Philadelphia Inquirer*, May 3, 2001, C:1, 7.

"E. Whiteland Developer Unveils Philadelphia Skyscraper Plans," *Daily Local News*, May 17, 2001, B:1, 4.

Henry J. Holcomb, "New Center City Skyscraper 'Will Rise Up in a Quiet Way,'" *Philadelphia Inquirer*, May 17, 2001, A:1, 4.

Harriet Lessy, "Rouse Plans $390 Million Skyscraper," *Philadelphia Daily News*, May 17, 2001, online addition.

John E. Czarnecki, "Stern to Scrape Philly Sky," *Architectural Record*, June 2001, 40.

Henry J. Holcomb, "Liberty Is Staying Suburban While Opening Office in Town," *Philadelphia Inquirer*, November 8, 2001, D:1, 2.

Dorie Baker, "For American Architects, the Sky Is Still the Limit, Says Stern," *Yale Bulletin & Calendar*, November 9, 2001, 3.

Sasha Issenberg, "Are Skyscrapers Obsolete?" *Philadelphia*, December 2001, 129, 162.

Roxanne Patel, "The House that Rouse Built," *Philadelphia*, December 2001, 126–29, 156, 158–63.

Michael Brick, "A Little Something for the Philadelphia Skyline," *New York Times*, May 29, 2002, C6.

Thomas J. Walsh, "New Designs on Philadelphia," *Urban Land*, October 2002, 142–49.

Residence and Office Building at Quartier am Tacheles
Berlin, Germany, 2000–

Partner: Paul L. Whalen. Senior Associate: Daniel Lobitz. Project Manager: Nancy Thiel. Senior Assistants: Jason Hwang, Qu Kim, Joel Mendelson, Julie Nymann. Assistants: Michiko Ashida, Johnny Cruz, Evanthia Dova, Patrick Hentsch-Cowles, Corina Rugeroni. Master Planner: Duany Plater-Zyberk & Company.

Rainer Haubrich, "New York braucht man nicht neu zu erfinden," *Die Welt*, April 25, 2001, 31.

Master Plan, Bryn Mawr School
Baltimore, Maryland, 2001–2002

Partner: Graham S. Wyatt. Senior Associate: Augusta Barone. Assistants: Fred Berthelot, Gary Brewer.

New Northrup Hall, Trinity University
San Antonio, Texas, 2000–2003

Partner: Alexander P. Lamis. Senior Associate: Adam Anuszkiewicz. Associate: Diane Scott-Burkin. Project Manager: Mike Soriano. Assistants: Giovanna Albretti, Jennifer Berlly, Lindsay Bishop, Josh Bull, Julia Katrin Buse, Marcus Carter, Dariel Cobb, Johnny Cruz, Enid DeGracia, Sara Evans, Yusung Hwang, Hyung Kee Lee, Edmund Leveckis, Thomas Manley, Ernesto Martinez, Jennifer Newsom, Marie-Faye Ngo, Nicolas Oudin, Salvador Peña-Figueroa, Mark Rodriguez, Ahmad-ali Sarder-Afkhami, Elise Seingier, Derek Willis, Ching-Chyi Yang, Siew Lee Yap. Landscape Associate: Marsh Kriplen. Landscape Assistants: Ashley Christopher, Thomas Fletcher. Interiors Assistants: Sharmell Anderson, Virginia Cornell, Vennie Lau, Kathleen Mancini. Local Architect: Kell Muñoz Architects.

"Buzz," *Architecture*, April 2001, 37.

"Architect Chosen, Contracts Signed, as Plans for New Northrup Progress," *Trinity*, Spring 2001, 7.

Amy Dorsett, "Trinity's Northrup Hall Coming Down," *San Antonio Express-News*, December 21, 2001, online edition.

Mike Greenberg, "Aesthetic Turf War?" *San Antonio Express-News*, December 23, 2001, online edition.

Stephan Sharpe, "Trinity Razes Ford's Original Building," *Texas Architect*, September–October 2002, 12.

Residence
East Hampton, New York, 2000–

Partner: Randy M. Correll. Project Manager: Mark Haladyna. Assistants: Marc Rehman, Derek Willis. Landscape Assistants: Ashley Christopher, Michael Weber.

Hickey Freeman Shop
666 Fifth Avenue, New York, New York, 2000–2001

Partner: Graham S. Wyatt. Senior Associate: John Gilmer. Project Manager: Jonas Goldberg. Senior Assistant: Tom Tulloch. Assistants: Ernesto Martinez, Hollace Metzger, Martin Russocki, Ahmad-ali Sarder-Afkhami, Richard Wachter. Interiors Assistants: Sharmell Anderson, Virginia Cornell, Fawn Galli, Kelly Greeson, Amie Haugh, Vennie Lau, Ken Stuckenschneider, Georgette Sturam, Joy Tucci.

"Top Projects of 1999: 666 Fifth Avenue," *New York Construction News*, June 2000, 38.

Stan Gellers, "Hickey-Freeman to Open Store on Fifth Avenue," *DNR*, November 29, 2000, 1.

Stan Gellers, "The Reinvention of Hickey-Freeman," *DNR*, March 23, 2001, 12, 14.

Main Library
Columbus, Georgia, 2001–

Partner: Alexander P. Lamis. Project Manager: Julie Nymann. Senior Assistant: Salvador Peña-Figueroa. Assistants: James Park, James Pearson, George Punnoose, Ahmad-Ali Sardar-Afkhami. Landscape Associate: Marsh Kriplen. Landscape Assistant: Michael Weber. Interiors Senior Associate: John Gilmer. Interior Assistants: Sharmell Anderson, Hyung Kee Lee. Associate Architect: Hecht, Burdeshaw, Johnson, Kidd and Clark Inc.

Mark Rice, "Architects Examined," *Columbus Ledger-Enquirer*, August 25, 2000, 1, 2.

Mark Rice, "Architect Is Selected for Columbus Library," *Columbus Ledger-Enquirer*, September 9, 2000, online edition.

Mark Rice, "Six Library Site Options Presented," *Columbus Ledger-Enquirer*, March 29, 2001, A:1.

Mark Rice, "Library's Master Site Plan Approved," *Columbus Ledger-Enquirer*, April 14, 2001, B:1.

Mark Rice, "Architect Shares Vision for Library," *Columbus Ledger-Enquirer*, April 22, 2001, A:1.

Mark Rice, "School Board to Vote on Plan Next Week," *Columbus Ledger-Enquirer*, April 23, 2001, C:1.

Mark Rice, "Master Plan," *Columbus Ledger-Enquirer*, April 24, 2001, online edition.

Michael Owen, "Critical Stage for New Library," *Columbus Ledger-Enquirer*, April 25, 2001, online edition.

Mark Rice, "Proposed Park Near Library Raises Questions," *Columbus Ledger-Enquirer*, May 1, 2001, online edition.

Mark Rice, "Library Plan Adds Public Space," *Columbus Ledger-Enquirer*, June 14, 2001, online edition.

Mark Rice, "Design Dazzles," *Columbus Ledger-Enquirer*, August 9, 2001, online edition.

Mark Rice, "First Look," *Columbus Ledger-Enquirer*, August 12, 2001, online edition.

Mark Rice, "Board Debates Library Roof," *Columbus Ledger-Enquirer*, August 14, 2001, online edition.

Mark Rice, "Group Approves Library Design," *Columbus Ledger-Enquirer*, August 15, 2001, online edition.

Mark Rice, "Board Passes Library Design," *Columbus Ledger-Enquirer*, August 21, 2001, online edition.

Mark Rice, "Three Plans Offered for Library Site," *Columbus Ledger-Enquirer*, August 22, 2001, online edition.

Michael Owen, "Build It to Last," *Columbus Ledger-Enquirer*, August 23, 2001, online edition.

Mark Rice, "New Library Faces Cuts," *Columbus Ledger-Enquirer*, September 11, 2001.

Mark Rice, "Library May Shrink 5 Percent," *Columbus Ledger-Enquirer*, November 30, 2001, online edition.

Mark Rice, "Panel OK's 5 Percent Cut in Library Size," *Columbus Ledger-Enquirer*, December 11, 2001, online edition.

Richard Hyatt, "Library Entry Plan Sparks Debate: Architects to Charge $39,000 for Covered Design," *Columbus Ledger-Enquirer*, February 26, 2002, online edition.

Holly Yan, "New Library to Have Cool Interior, Dude," *Columbus Ledger-Enquirer*, August 7, 2002, C:4.

Education and Visitors Center, Mark Twain House
Hartford, Connecticut, 2000–2003

Partner: Graham S. Wyatt. Senior Associate: Kevin Smith. Associate: Dennis Sagiev. Senior Assistant: Kurt Glauber. Assistants: Enid DeGracia, John Ellis, Jennifer Rice, Ole Sondresen.

Ken Dixon, "New Center to Join Twain's 'Dream House,'" *Connecticut Post*, November 16, 2000.

"Finally, Twain at Center Stage," *Hartford Courant*, November 16, 2000.

Gregory B. Hladky, "Yale Dean to Design Mark Twain Center," *New Haven Register*, November 16, 2000, A:3, 5.

Frances Grandy Taylor, "Yale Dean Relishes Twain Architectural Project," *Hartford Courant*, November 17, 2000, 1–3.

Natasha Gural, "Architect with Sense of Humor to Do Twain Project," *Bergen Record*, November 19, 2000.

Laurie Ledgard, "'Worthy of the Almighty' and Robert Stern," *Hartford Business Journal*, November 20, 2000, 1, 16.

"Off the Record," *Architectural Record*, February 2001, 32.

Mike Swift, "Architectural Wonders," *Northeast* (Sunday magazine, *Hartford Courant*), March 11, 2001, 1, 5–9, 13.

586

Stacey Stowe, "Architectural Superstars Tackle Three Hartford Attractions," *New York Times*, July 29, 2001, Connecticut edition, 14:7.

Tom Puleo, "A Novel Design: Big Plans Unveiled for Low-Key Visitor Center at Twain House," *Hartford Courant*, November 16, 2001, B:1, 2.

Eleanor Charles, "Visitors' Center to Be Built at Mark Twain House," *New York Times*, January 20, 2002, 11:9.

Bill Clegg, "Designed for a Successful Future," *Hartford Courant*, February 16, 2002, A:10.

Tom Puleo, "Hopes that Disney and Twain Shall Meet," *Hartford Courant*, February 16, 2002.

"From Mickey to Mark," *Hartford Courant*, February 17, 2002, C:2.

Tom Puleo and Carrie Budoff, "Twain Folks Like Idea of Mouse in the House," *Hartford Courant*, February 20, 2002, online edition.

United States Courthouse
Richmond, Virginia, 2001–2006

Partner: Grant F. Marani. Project Manager: Paul Zembsch. Assistants: Marcus Carter, Eric Hofmann, Susannah Jackson, Charles Toothill. Interiors Senior Assistant: Ken Stuckenschneider. Interiors Assistant: Sharmell Anderson. Associate Architect: HLM Design.

Alan Cooper, "Seventh-Broad Site for Courthouse?" *Richmond Times-Dispatch*, October 11, 2001, B:5.

Alan Cooper and Will Jones, "Courthouse to Be Built Downtown," *Richmond Times-Dispatch*, February 16, 2002, B:1, 4.

Tom Campbell, "U.S. Courthouse Design Coming," *Richmond Times-Dispatch*, November 11, 2002, B:4 .

Tom Campbell, "Courthouse to Fit Setting," *Richmond Times-Dispatch*, November 16, 2002, B:4.

Edwin Slipek Jr., "Order in the Court," *Style Weekly*, December 4, 2002, 35.

Torre Almirante
Avenida Almirante Barroso, Rio de Janeiro, Brazil, 2001–2004

Partner: Graham Wyatt. Senior Associate: Meghan McDermott. Senior Assistant: Don Lee. Assistants: Giovanni Albretti, Daniel Arbelaez, Flavia Bueno, Leonid Khanin, Ernesto Martinez. Associate Architect: Pontual Arquitetura.

"The Road to Rio," *Hinesight*, October–December 2002, 3.

Jacksonville Public Library
Jacksonville, Florida, 2001–2004

Partner: Alexander P. Lamis. Project Manager: James Pearson. Project Architect: Jeffery Povero. Assistants: Giovanna Albretti, Adam Anuszkiewicz, Johnny Cruz, Kevin Fitzgerald, Thomas Fletcher, Mark Gage, Anthony Goldsby, Salvador Peña-Figueroa, George Punnoose. Landscape Associate: Marsh Kriplen. Landscape Assistant: Ashley Christopher. Interiors Assistants: Virginia Cornell, Kathleen Mancini. Local Architect: Rolland, DelValle & Bradley.

P. Douglas Filaroski, "Library Officials Approve Four Firms to Submit Designs," *Florida Times-Union*, June 14, 2001, B:1, 8.

Susanna Barton, "Having Designs on Jacksonville's New Library," *Business Journal*, June 15, 2001, online edition.

Susanna Barton, "A New Chapter: City Takes Page from National Design Firms," *Business Journal*, June 22–28, 2001, 1, 44.

P. Douglas Filaroski, "Architects Vie to Design New Jacksonville Library," *Florida Times-Union*, July 12, 2001, online edition.

"Gentlemen, Start Your Drawing," *Florida Times-Union*, July 12, 2001, online edition.

P. Douglas Filaroski, "Nashville's Novel Idea a Preview for Jacksonville," *Florida Times-Union*, July 20, 2001, A:1, 13.

P. Douglas Filaroski, "New Library Must Deal with Past," *Florida Times-Union*, August 4, 2001, B:1, 3.

"Record News," *Architectural Record*, August 2001, 32.

David Bauerlein, "Architects Ready Library Plans: Final Decision to Come This Week," *Florida Times-Union*, December 16, 2001, online edition.

"Jacksonville Public Library Proposals," *Florida Times-Union*, December 16, 2001.

"Which Rendering of the Library Do You Like Best?" *Florida Times-Union*, December 17, 2001, online edition.

David Bauerlein, "Library Plans All Exceed Budget: Architects Present Four Designs to City Experts," *Florida Times-Union*, December 18, 2001, online edition.

David Bauerlein, "City's New Main Library Will Have Classical Look: Delaney Expected to OK Panel's Pick," *Florida Times-Union*, December 19, 2001, online edition.

David Bauerlein, "Library Analysis under Fire: Designers Question Estimates of Costs," *Florida Times-Union*, December 20, 2001, online edition.

David Bauerlein, "Stern Library Design Rises to Top: Mayor Accepts Committee's Pick," *Florida Times-Union*, December 21, 2001, online edition.

David DeCamp, "Donors to Fund Library Perks?" *Florida Times-Union*, December 21, 2001, online edition.

David Bauerlein, "Library Design Firm Faces Fine: Group Not Cleared for Florida Business," *Florida Times-Union*, December 22, 2001, online edition.

William A. Leuthold, "Library: Classical Design Is Timeless," *Florida Times-Union*, December 25, 2001, online edition.

James O. Kemp, "Architecture: Only Architects Are Qualified to Judge," *Florida Times-Union*, January 1, 2002, online edition.

Robert Tebbs, "Library: Design Is Disappointing," *Florida Times-Union*, January 2, 2002, online edition.

Matthew W. Smith, "Architects: Elitist Attitude Is Hard to Swallow," *Florida Times-Union*, January 3, 2002, online edition.

"Architecture: For Everyone," *Florida Times-Union*, January 6, 2002, online edition.

Clyde Jennings, "Library: Design Choice Is Perfect," *Florida Times-Union*, January 6, 2002, online edition.

Robert Woolverton, "Library: Wrong Design Was Chosen," *Florida Times-Union*, January 6, 2002, online edition.

Prakash Desai, "Library: Let Local Architects Vote," *Florida Times-Union*, January 7, 2002, online edition.

Paul Z. Fletcher, "Library: Classical Design Is Perfect," *Florida Times-Union*, January 7, 2002, online edition.

John Falconetti, "Library: Facility Will Be Work of Art," *Florida Times-Union*, January 10, 2002, online edition.

Ted Pappas, "Library: Concept Will Be an Asset," *Florida Times-Union*, January 10, 2002, online edition.

David Bauerlein, "Library Design Firm Must Pay Fine," *Florida Times-Union*, February 9, 2002, online edition.

"Main Library Will Feature Exciting, Vibrant Atmosphere," *Business Journal*, February 15, 2002, 11.

Stanley Collyer, "Budget Questions in Jacksonville," *Competitions*, Spring 2002, 6–33.

David Bauerlein, "Library Designer Goes for Useful, Historic," *Florida Times-Union*, December 16, 2002, online edition.

David Bauerlein, "City Looks to Future," *Florida Times-Union*, December 17, 2002, online edition.

The Plaza at PPL Center
Allentown, Pennsylvania, 2001–2003

Partner: Graham S. Wyatt. Senior Associate: Meghan McDermott. Associate: Kevin O'Connor. Project Manager: Breen Mahony. Assistants: Fred Berthelot, Leonid Khanin, Ernesto Martinez, William Smith, David Vimont, Lindsay Weiss, Ching-Chyi Yang. Landscape Associate: Marsh Kriplen. Landscape Assistants: Christina Belton, Michael Weber, Mei Wu. Interiors Assistant: Sharmell Anderson. Associate Architect: Kendall/Heaton Associates.

Dan Hartzell, "PPL Project Has Doubled in Size," *Morning Call* (Allentown), September 8, 2001.

Henry J. Holcomb, "Rouse Office Building Is Planned for Allentown," *Philadelphia Inquirer*, November 15, 2001, online edition.

Bob Wittman, "PPL Ready to Expand under Glass," *Morning Call*, November 15, 2001.

"A New Building, New Promise for Allentown: Solutions Livable Cities," *Morning Call*, November 18, 2001, A:20.

Bob Wittman, "Businesses Show Interest in Downtown Site," *Morning Call*, November 29, 2001, B:1, 8.

Ann Wlazelek, "Emmaus Grad Built PPL Model," *Morning Call*, November 29, 2001, B:4.

Bob Wittman, "PPL Plaza Design Is Clean, Green," *Morning Call*, September 18, 2002, A:1, 4.

"PPL Building: Lighter Shades of Green," *Officeinsight*, February 17, 2003, 9.

Bob Wittman, "Herbs to Blossom into PPL Roof Garden," *Morning Call*, May 15, 2003, B:3.

Bob Wittman, "Plaza at PPL Opens New Era Today," *Morning Call*, June 19, 2003, A:1, 8, 9.

Inga Saffron, "Truly Green and Distinctly Urban, Rouse Building Graces Allentown," *Philadelphia Inquirer*, Friday, June 20, 2003, E:1, 4.

Bob Wittman, "PPL Building Dedication Is a Veritable Fountain of Hope," *Morning Call*, June 20, 2003, A:1.

One St. Thomas Street
Toronto, Ontario, Canada, 2001–

Partner: Paul L. Whalen. Associate: Hernán Chebar. Assistants: Thomas Tulloch, Richard Wachter. Associate Architect: Young + Wright Architects.

Christopher Hume, "Stern Stuff," *Toronto Star*, May 4, 2002, P:1, 10.

Therese Bissell, "Then We Take Toronto," *Nuvo*, Spring 2003, 44–46.

Smeal College of Business Administration, Pennsylvania State University
State College, Pennsylvania, 2001–

Partner: Graham Wyatt. Senior Associate: Kevin Smith. Project Manager: Enid DeGracia, Jonas Goldberg. Senior Assistant: Gregory Christopher. Assistants: Jennifer Berlly, Fred Berthelot, Alex Butler, Kevin Fitzgerald, Ryan Rodenberg, Sue Sung, Lindsay Weiss. Associate Architect: Bower Lewis Thrower.

Jason Fagone, "Building Boom," *Penn Stater*, January–February 2003, 28–35.

Philadelphia Naval Business Center
Philadelphia, Pennsylvania, Competition, 2002

Partner: Graham Wyatt. Associate: Kevin O'Connor. Senior Assistants: Don Lee, Jack Robbins. Assistants: Dariel Cobb, Jennifer Rice, Robie Wood. Land Planner: EDAW. Associate Architect: Kelly/Maiello.

Henry J. Holcomb, "Rouse's Firm Wins Navy Base Contract, Where the City Hopes to Create Jobs," *Philadelphia Inquirer*, August 16, 2002, online edition.

Henry J. Holcomb, "Liberty Plans Seventy-Acre Office Park and More," *Philadelphia Inquirer*, February 19, 2003, D:1, 3.

Meadowlands Master Plan
Lyndhurst, Rutherford, and North Arlington, New Jersey, 2002–

Partner: Paul L. Whalen. Senior Associate: Daniel Lobitz. Project Manager: Joel Mendelson. Assistants: Rob Polacek, Can Tiryaki.

John Holusha, "For Developers, Brownfields Look Less Risky," *New York Times*, April 21, 2002, 11:1, 6.

Master Plan
Heiligendamm, Germany, 2002–

Partner: Paul L. Whalen. Senior Associate: Daniel Lobitz. Project Manager: Chris Pizzi. Assistants: Evanthia Dova, Jason Hwang, David MacPhail.

Resort de Veneguera
Gran Canaria, Canary Islands, Spain, Competition, 2002

Partner: Paul L. Whalen. Senior Associate: Daniel Lobitz. Project Manager: Nancy Thiel. Senior Assistants: Mark Gage, Joel Mendelson, Chris Pizzi, Can Tiryaki. Assistants: Ceren Bingol, Flavia Bueno, Rob Polacek, Mark Rodriguez, Richard Wachter. Landscape Associate: Marsh Kriplen. Landscape Senior Assistant: Michael Weber. Landscape Assistant: Ming Te Kang.

Additional Projects

Addition to House at Apaquogue
East Hampton, New York, 2000–2001

Partner: Randy M. Correll. Assistant: Molly Denver.

Robert A. M. Stern: Buildings and Projects, 1987–1992, introduction by Vincent Scully (New York: Rizzoli, 1992), 322–23.

Nicholas Shrady, "An American Beauty: Colonial Profile for an East Hampton Residence," *Architectural Digest*, December 1995, 160–65, 201.

Robert A. M. Stern: Houses (New York: The Monacelli Press, 1997), 584–605.

Robert A. M. Stern: Buildings and Projects, 1993–1998 (New York: The Monacelli Press, 1998), 58–63.

House Renovation
Bel Air, California, 2000–2001

Partner: Roger H. Seifter. Associate Partner: Arthur Chabon. Project Manager: Lenore Passavanti. Assistants: Roxanna Klein-Rosenkranz, Clemenstien Love, Robert Miller, Karen Stonely, Elizabeth Valella.

International Storytelling Center
Jonesborough, Tennessee, 1996–2002

Partner: Paul L. Whalen. Senior Associate: Gary Brewer. Associate: Christine Kelley. Associate Architect: Ken Ross Architects, Inc.

Robert A. M. Stern: Buildings and Projects, 1993–1998 (New York: The Monacelli Press, 1998), 308–9.

Lesia Paine-Brooks, "Ground Broken for New Storytelling Facility," *Johnson City Press*, July 1, 1999, 1, 8.

James Brooks, "Storytelling Center Opening Thursday," *Johnson City Press*, June 16, 2002.

Jennifer Lawson, "Storytelling Center Attracts Thousands," *Knoxville News-Sentinel*, December 27, 2003, A:1, 10.

Santa Monica UCLA Medical Center/Orthopaedic Hospital Replacement Project
Santa Monica, California, 1997–2007

Partner: Paul L. Whalen. Associates: Diane Scott Burkin, Thu Do, Yuri Zagorin. Assistants: Johnny Cruz, Carmen Gonzalez, Sara Ridenour. Associate Architects: Anshen + Allen.

Linda Y. Kalama, "New Hospital Plans Unveiled," *At Your Hospital*, September 1999, 13–17.

Yonkers Public Library and Board of Education Offices
Yonkers, New York, 1998

Partner: Alexander P. Lamis. Project Manager: Gordon Cousins. Senior Associate: Daniel Lobitz. Senior Assistant: Salvador Peña-Figueroa. Assistants: John Ellis, Michael Flaherty, Michael Wilbur.

Len Maniace, "In Yonkers, a Waterfront Plan—at Last," *Journal News*, January 13, 1999, Westchester edition, B:1, 2.

Len Maniace, "Desegregation Ruling Jeopardizes School Project," *Journal News*, June 29, 1999, Yonkers/Hudson River edition, B:3.

Len Maniace, "Yonkers Shelves Library's Architect," *Journal News*, Yonkers/Hudson River edition, April 12, 2000, B:1, 7.

Accessories
Valli & Valli, 1998–2002

Partner: Paul L. Whalen. Senior Associate: John Gilmer. Project Designers: Peter Fleming, Nancy Thiel. Assistants: Kimberly Raspanti, Richard Wachter.

Residence in Forest Hill
Toronto, Ontario, 1998

Partner: Roger H. Seifter. Senior Assistant: Victoria Baran.

Morris Quadrangle Corporate Campus
Florham Park, New Jersey, 1998–

Partner: Graham S. Wyatt. Project Designers/Managers: Gregory Christopher, Enid DeGracia, Frank de Santis. Assistants: Zvi Gersh, James Johnson.

Addition to Enron Corporate Headquarters
Houston, Texas, Competition, 1998

Partner: Graham S. Wyatt. Associate Partner: Barry Rice. Senior Assistants: Anselm Fusco, Dennis Sagiev. Assistants: Johnny Cruz, John Mueller.

425 Fifth Avenue
New York, New York, 1998

Partner: Alexander P. Lamis. Associate Partner: Barry Rice. Associate: Michael D. Jones. Project Manager: Hernán Chebar. Senior Assistants: Anselm Fusco, Dennis Sagiev. Assistants: John Esposito, Ken Glazer, Alexander Karmeinsky, Ernesto Leon. Associate Architect: H. Thomas O'Hara Architect.

Alan S. Oser, "A Rental Builder Shifts to High Gear," *New York Times*, June 21, 1998, 11:1, 6.

Edwin McDowell, "Around Grand Central, New Office Towers and a Fifty-Four-Floor Residence," *New York Times*, February 13, 2000, 11:1, 6.

"Fifty-Four-Story Building Going Up at Fifth Avenue and Thirty-Eighth Street: Change of Big-Name Architect," *New York Times*, August 12, 2001, 11:1.

311 Bay Street
Toronto, Canada, 1998

Partner: Paul L. Whalen. Associate Partner: Barry Rice. Associate: Michael Jones. Assistants: Hernán Chebar, Breen Mahony. Associate Architect: Beinhaker Irwin Associates.

Performing Arts Center, Proctor Academy
Andover, New Hampshire, 1998

Partner: Graham Wyatt. Project Architect: Adam Anuszkiewicz. Assistant: Alex Karmeinsky.

Wave Hill Chair
Riverdale, The Bronx, New York, 2000

Senior Associate: Gary Brewer. Assistant: Fawn Galli.

Meetinghouse Golf Club
Edgartown, Martha's Vineyard, Massachusetts, 1998

Partner: Graham S. Wyatt. Associate Partner: Grant F. Marani. Senior Assistant: Douglas Wright. Assistant: Andrei Martin. Landscape Associate: Dawn Handler. Landscape Assistants: Katherine Bennett, Sung Ok.

"Playing through the Claptrap," *Martha's Vineyard Times*, May 13, 1999, 16.

Gingerbread House for the *New York Times Magazine*
1998

Partner: Roger H. Seifter. Senior Assistant: Victoria Baran.

Pilar Viladas, "A Home for the Holidays," *New York Times Magazine*, December 20, 1998, 78–79.

Broad Center for the Biological Sciences, California Institute of Technology
Pasadena, California, Competition, 1998

Partner: Graham S. Wyatt. Senior Assistants: Marina Berendeeva, Dennis Sagiev. Assistant: Alex Karmeinsky.

Presidio Village
San Francisco, California, Competition, 1998

Partner: Paul L. Whalen. Senior Associate: Daniel Lobitz. Senior Assistant: Joel Mendelson. Assistants: Michael McClure, Emily Stegner. Associate Architect: Gensler.

Gerald D. Adams, "All Four Presidio Plans Fall Short, Report Concludes," *San Francisco Examiner*, April 21, 1999, 1.

Sasha Cavender, "Deciding the Destiny of a Twenty-Three-Acre Universe," *New York Times*, May 23, 1999, 3:2.

Sara Hart, "Lucasfilm in Bid to Develop Presidio," *Architecture*, May 1999, 41.

55 East Erie
Chicago, Illinois, 1999

Associate Partner: Barry Rice. Associate: Michael Jones. Assistants: Hernán Chebar, Zvi Gersh, Dennis Giobbe, Ernesto Leon. Landscape Associate: Dawn Handler. Associate Architect: Fujikawa Johnson and Associates.

Residence
Pacific Palisades, California, 1999

Partner: Roger H. Seifter. Associate: Michael Jones.

De Taats
Utrecht, The Netherlands, 1999–

Partner: Paul L. Whalen. Senior Associate: Daniel Lobitz. Associate: Hernán Chebar. Assistants: John Esposito, Qu Kim, Ernesto Leon, Corina Rugeroni, Diane Scott, Michael Soriano. Landscape Associate: Marsh Kriplen. Associate Architect: Inbo Architects.

House Renovation
San Francisco, California, 1999–2000

Partner: Roger H. Seifter. Senior Assistant: Elise Geiger. Landscape Senior Assistant: Ashley Christopher. Interior Designer: Eugenia Jesberg Interior Design.

Disney's Beach Club Villas, Walt Disney World Resort
Lake Buena Vista, Florida, 1999–2002

Partner: Paul L. Whalen. Associate: Douglas Wright. Project Architect: Sargent Gardiner. Assistant: Julie Nymann. Associate Architect: KBJ Architects.

Apartment in the Chatham
New York, New York, 1999–2001

Partner: Grant F. Marani. Senior Assistant: Deborah Wilen-Cohen. Assistant: Chuck Toothill.

House and Guest Cottage
Sonoma County, California, 1999–

Partner: Grant F. Marani. Senior Assistants: Mark Pledger, Rebecca Post. Assistants: Catharine Dayal, Elise Geiger, Qu Kim.

Residence
Woodside, California, 1999

Partner: Grant F. Marani. Associate: Christine Kelley. Assistant: Elena Bresciani.

Guest Cottage at Siansconset
Nantucket, Massachusetts, 1999–

Partner: Grant F. Marani. Associate: Christine Kelley. Assistants: Catharine Dayal, Laura Hinton, Steve Petrides. Interiors Associate: Scott Sloat. Interiors Assistants: Thu Do, Joy Tucci.

Residence
San Francisco, California, 1999–

Partner: Grant F. Marani. Senior Assistants: Rebecca Post, Charles Toothill. Assistants: Catharine Dayal, Eric Hofmann, Gabriel Traupman.

Emily Howe Memorial Library
Hanover, New Hampshire, 1999–

Partner: Alexander P. Lamis. Project Manager/Designer: Salvador Peña-Figueroa. Assistants: Johnny Cruz, Julie Nymann, Jong-Hyuck Park. Landscape Associate: Dawn Handler. Landscape Assistant: Norbert Holter.

Alex Leary, "Howe Library Looking to Grow," *Valley News* (Hanover, New Hampshire), A:1, 5.

Residence at Squibnocket
Chilmark, Martha's Vineyard, Massachusetts, 1999

Associate Partner: Randy M. Correll.

Residence
Westport, Connecticut, 1999–

Associate Partner: Gary Brewer. Assistant: Christina Spaulding.

Colorado Christian University
Lakewood, Colorado, Competition, 1999

Partner: Graham S. Wyatt. Associate Partner: Grant F. Marani. Associate: Anselm Fusco. Assistant: Dennis Sagiev.

Campus Center, Indiana University/Purdue University
Indianapolis, Indiana, 2000

Partner: Graham S. Wyatt. Senior Associate: Adam Anuszkiewicz. Associate: Kevin Smith. Assistants: Meredith Colon, Gordon Cousins, Anselm Fusco, Andrei Martin, Ernesto Martinez, Jack Robbins, Dennis Sagiev, Ahmad-ali Sarder-Afkhami, Carol Dufresne Trent.

Tuhaye
Park City, Utah, 2001–

Partner: Paul L. Whalen. Senior Associate: Daniel Lobitz. Project Manager: Nancy Thiel. Senior Assistants: Gaylin Bowie, Joel Mendelson, Julie Nymann, Rosalind Tsang. Assistants: Michiko Ashida, Evanthia Dova, Rob Polacek, Corina Rugeroni.

Residence on Maui
Kapalua, Hawaii, 1999

Partner: Grant F. Marani. Associate: Douglas Wright. Senior Assistant: Pamela McGirr. Assistant: Kimberly Raspanti. Interiors Senior Associate: John Gilmer. Landscape Assistant: Mei Wu.

School of Business, College of William and Mary
Williamsburg, Virginia, 1999–

Partner: Graham S. Wyatt. Associate: Kevin Smith. Senior Assistant: Melissa DelVecchio. Assistants: Fred Berthelot, Oscar Sanchez, Sean Tobin, Carol Dufresne Trent. Associate Architect: Marcellus Wright Cox & Smith Architects.

Residence
Fort Washington, Pennsylvania, 2000

Partner: Randy M. Correll. Landscape Assistant: Norbert Holter.

UCLA Cancer Center, Westwood Campus, University of California, Los Angeles
Los Angeles, California, 2000

Partner: Paul L. Whalen. Project Manager: Kevin O'Connor. Senior Assistant: Sara Ridenour. Associate Architect: RBB Architects, Inc.

Residence
Ross, California, 2000–

Partner: Roger H. Seifter. Senior Assistants: Dennis Giobbe, David Solomon.

"Udderly Delightful"
Cow Parade, West Orange, New Jersey, 2000

Partner: Alexander P. Lamis. Senior Associate: Daniel Lobitz. Senior Assistants: Michael Combs, Daniel Wolfskehl. Assistants: Travis Field, Chris Gonya, Roy Griffith, Chris Hall, Harry Kim, Joel Mendelson, Jennifer Morris, Hiro Shimizu, Joy Tucci.

John Kifner, "Rather See than Be One: Bovine Art that Takes Some Getting Used To," *New York Times*, May 9, 2000, B:1.

Dan Bischoff, "West Orange Cow Parade 2000 Showcases Bovine Art—and Really Bad Puns," *Star Ledger*, June 23–29, 2000, Ticket section, 27.

Andrew Jacobs, "West Orange: Cavalcade of Cows," *New York Times*, June 26, 2000, B:4.

Snowmass Base Village
Snowmass, Colorado, Competition, 2000

Partners: Paul L. Whalen, Graham S. Wyatt. Senior Associate: Daniel Lobitz. Project Manager: Nancy Thiel. Senior Assistants: John Cays, Gregory Christopher, Joel Mendelson. Assistants: Evanthia Dova, Chris Hall, Gregory Horgan, Jason Hwang, Martin Russocki.

Pequot Library
Southport, Connecticut, 2000

Partner: Alexander P. Lamis. Project Managers: Julie Nymann, Salvador Peña-Figueroa. Assistants: Alex Barker, Julia Buse, Marcus Carter, Yusung Hwang, Tae Kim, Ernesto Martinez, Jennifer Newsom, Ahmad-ali Sarder-Afkhami, Elise Seingier, Derek Willis, Daniel Wolfskehl, Siew Lee Yap.

Town Center, DC Ranch
Scottsdale, Arizona, 2000

Partner: Paul L. Whalen. Senior Associate: Daniel Lobitz. Project Manager: Nancy Thiel. Assistants: Evanthia Dova, Joel Mendelson, Julie Nymann.

55 Railroad Avenue
Greenwich, Connecticut, 2000–2003

Partner: Graham S. Wyatt. Senior Associate: Adam Anuszkiewicz. Project Managers: Gregory Christopher, Thomas Salazar. Assistants: Jennifer Berlly, Fred Berthelot, Marcus Carter, Enid DeGracia, John Ellis, Qu Kim, Jack Robbins, Corina Rugeroni, Ahmad-ali Sarder-Afkhami. Landscape Associate: Marsh Kriplen. Landscape Assistant: Christina Belton.

Peter Healy, "Railroad Avenue Building Gets Makeover," *Greenwich Time*, January 8, 2002, B:7, 8.

Sana Siwolop, "Greenwich Offices, and Rents, Are Sprucing Up," *New York Times*, June 5, 2002, C:5.

Campus Center, College of Notre Dame of Maryland
Baltimore, Maryland, 2000

Partner: Graham S. Wyatt. Senior Associate: Augusta Barone. Assistant: Jennifer Rice.

Townhouses on Liberty Street
Frisco Square, Frisco, Texas, 2000–2004

Partner: Paul L. Whalen. Senior Associate: Daniel Lobitz. Project Manager: Nancy Thiel. Senior Assistant: Jason Hwang. Assistants: Veronica Caminos, Yusung Hwang, Richard Wachter, Derek Willis.

Apartment Building for Parcel 19B
Battery Park City, New York, New York, 2000–

Partner: Paul L. Whalen. Associate: Hernán Chebar. Assistants: Qu Kim, Corina Rugeroni. Associate Architect: Ismael Leyva Architects.

Rachelle Garbarine, "Enclave Turns Green, Inside and Out," *New York Times*, March 23, 2001, B:7.

Charles David, "The Green Big Apple," *Urban Land*, Spring 2001, 17–19, 38.

Office Building
Centre du Val d'Europe, Marne-la-Vallée, France, 2000–

Partner: Paul L. Whalen. Project Architect: Kevin O'Connor. Assistant: Evanthia Dova. Associate Architect: Inter Faces.

Master Plan and Student Center, Hopkins School
New Haven, Connecticut, 2000

Partner: Graham S. Wyatt. Senior Associate: Gary Brewer. Assistants: Dana Gulling, Christina Spaulding.

Folie Bergère
Parrish Art Museum exhibition "Follies: Fantasy in the Landscape," 2001

Senior Associate: Daniel Lobitz. Assistant: Martin Russocki.

Cottage
Carmel, California, 2001–

Partner: Grant F. Marani. Associate: Douglas Wright. Project Manager: Pamela McGirr. Senior Assistant: Rebecca Post. Assistant: Kimberly Raspanti. Interiors Senior Assistant: Virginia Cornell. Interiors Assistant: Paula Velazquez. Landscape Associate: Marsh Kriplen. Landscape Assistant: Christina Belton.

Simons Center for the Arts, College of Charleston
Charleston, South Carolina, 2001–

Partner: Alexander P. Lamis. Senior Associate: Gary Brewer. Associate Architect: Stevens & Wilkinson of South Carolina.

Robert Behre, "Design Center to Help College in Simons Center Impasse," *Post & Courier* (Charleston), January 30, 2003, online edition.

Robert Behre, "Meeting Fails to Clear Up Simons Center Impasse," *Post & Courier*, February 3, 2003, B:1, 5.

Jason Hardin "The BAR Tastes Too Modern for Old City, Critics Argue," *Post & Courier*, February 5, 2003, online edition.

Residence at One Central Park
New York, New York, 2001

Partner: Paul L. Whalen. Senior Associates: John Gilmer, Daniel Lobitz. Project Manager: Nancy Thiel. Interiors Assistant: Kelly Greeson.

Mildred F. Schmertz, "One Central Park Tower: Robert A. M. Stern and Thad Hayes Envision Singular Spaces for a Manhattan High-Rise," *Architectural Digest*, October 2002, 152–56.

Residence on Sunset Boulevard
Beverly Hills, California, 2001

Partner: Roger H. Seifter. Project Manager: Rosa Maria Colina. Senior Assistant: Troy Curry. Assistant: Glenn Albrecht.

Columbus Seniors Center
Columbus, Indiana, 2001–

Partner: Graham Wyatt. Senior Associate: Kevin Smith. Project Manager: Jonas Goldberg. Senior Assistant: Gregory Christopher.

Brian Blair, "Council Members Hesitate on Senior Center," *Republic* (Columbus, Indiana), February 7, 2002, B:1.

Apartment Building
Larchmont, New York, 2002–

Partner: Paul L. Whalen. Senior Associate: Gary Brewer. Assistant: Richard Wachter. Associate Architect: SLCE Architects.

David Novich, "Developer Scales Back Plan for Apartments," *Journal News*, February 9, 2002, 3B.

John Holusha, "New Vitality around Old Railroad Stations," *New York Times*, March 16, 2003, 11:1–6.

Residence at Hubbard's Woods
Winnetka, Illinois, 2002–

Partner: Randy M. Correll. Project Manager: Daniel Teske. Senior Assistant: Haven Knight. Assistants: Sam O'Meara, David Vimont.

Residence on Bel Air Road
Los Angeles, California, 2002–

Partner: Roger H. Seifter. Associate: Victoria Baran. Assistants: Josh Coleman, Troy Curry, Chris McIntire.

Baker Library Academic Center, Harvard Business School
Boston, Massachusetts, 2002–2005

Partners: Alexander P. Lamis, Graham S. Wyatt. Senior Associate: Kevin Smith. Project Architect: Melissa DelVecchio. Project Manager: Kurt Glauber. Senior Assistants: Mark Gage, Donald Johnson. Assistants: Giovanna Albretti, Enid DeGracia, Sara Evans, Mark Haladyna, Thomas Salazar. Interiors Senior Assistant: Ken Stuckenschneider. Interiors Assistant: Nadine Holzheimer. Associate Architect: Finegold Alexander + Associates.

Adriana Boden, "Baker Library: A Renovation in the Making," *HARBUS* (student newspaper, Harvard Business School), May 5, 2003, 1, 3, 5.

Illustration Credits

592

Photography
Peter Aaron/Esto: 12–25, 27–41, 42–55, 57–67, 89–105, 118–31, 132–43, 152–61, 177–85, 236–41, 244–45, 256–62, 264–69, 278–85, 286–93, 294–99, 300–305, 307–17, 318–19, 321–33, 334–39, 364–65 (2), 366–84, 396–401, 410–17, 428–37, 438–49, 450–55, 462–75, 478–79, 480 (2), 481, 482 (5), 483 (7), 484 (9), 485, 486 (13), 487, 490–95, 518–23, 560 (3), 564 (3); courtesy of *Architectural Digest*, The Conde Nast Publications Inc.: 70–71 (3), 72–87, 106–17, 144–51, 198–223, 340–45; © The Walt Disney Company, used with permission: 186–93

Joe Aker/Aker Zvonkovic Photography: 228–35, 358 (2), 359–63, 534–35

Andre Baranowski: 350–55

Steven Brooke: 162–75, 246–53, 560 (1)

The Coastal Group: 392

© HBF, used with permission: 393

© Hines, used with permission: 255

Hoachlander David Photography: 224

© J. C. Decaux, used with permission: 276

Alex MacLean, Landslides: 320

Peter Mauss/Esto: 263

Robert Miller: 242–43

Jock Pottle/Esto: 347, 387, 419, 456–57, 560 (5), 561 (1, 3), 567 (4)

Marvin Rand: 270–75

James Wojcik: 562 (5)

Renderings
Advanced Media Design: 496–97, 504–5, 532–33, 561 (4)

Ernest Burden III: 276–77, 348–49, 408–9, 426–27, 489, 507–9, 555–57, 560 (4), 562 (2), 563 (4, 5), 567 (5), 569 (1)

Keith Hornblower: 477 (3, 5, 7, 9)

John Mason: 388 (3), 561 (2), 564 (4, 5), 565 (4), 567 (1, 3a), 568 (4), 569 (3), 570 (1, 5)

Michael McCann: 69, 390–91, 511–13, 527–28, 544–45, 553, 563 (2), 565 (3), 568 (1)

Andre Mellone: 567 (3), 568 (2)

Thomas Schaller: 225, 388 (1, 2), 389, 395, 405, 500–501, 515, 525, 531, 536–41, 543, 546–47, 550–51, 566 (5), 569 (2), 570 (4), 571 (3)

Clark Smith: 402–3, 407, 420–21, 424–25, 460–61, 516–17, 562 (4), 564 (2), 566 (4), 567 (3b), 570 (2), 571 (1, 2)

Dick Sneary: 549

Curtis Woodhouse: 356–57

Vladis Yeliseyev: 568 (3)

Editor's Acknowledgments

This book would not have been possible without the efforts of many people. I owe a debt of gratitude to those who worked with me to gather the images and to coordinate the text: Rachel Bright, Lisa Melyn Miller, and in particular, Robyne Walker Murphy. I also want to express my appreciation for the ongoing dedication of the other members of the External Communications Department at Robert A. M. Stern Architects: Mac Brydon, Rachel Cannon, Anita Franchetti, Jonathan Grzywacz, Harjit Jaiswal, and Shalik Rhynes. —P.M.D.